the
boy
who
fell

a wild stillness
publication

felix maus

the
boy
who
fell

by
mark alan lilly

a Father's Memoir
of Love, Community, Healing
(and a Fall from a Tree)

Wild Stillness

ISBN: 978-0989174107

First edition complete: 2:27pm, 05 October, 2013

First published: March 31, 2014

Final manuscript uploaded from the hallway outside the PICU.

TheBoyWhoFell.com

Table of Contents

This book is dedicated
to Felix, Hanna, Saskia and Tina,
to Simone,
and to the girl in the red cherry dress.

welcome

i have a story.

...let's say
it was 43 trillion cells
give or take a few,
that were busy that day
being the body
that held the soul
endearingly known
(to his father at least)
as Felix Maus.

SPRINGTIME!

It is strange to be here. The mystery never leaves you alone. Behind your image, below your words, above your thoughts, the silence of another world waits. A world lives within you. No one else can bring you news of this inner world. Through the opening of the mouth, we bring out sounds from the mountain beneath the soul. These sounds are words. The world is full of words.

JOHN O'DONOHUE, ANAM ĊARA

STRUNG TOGETHER

The words i wrote that summer that fill this memoir were a lifeline, an anchor to the unbroken. During the gravest time of my life i found footing to move through the pain that came our way.

While my son Felix faced death comatose in ICU, these words snatched for me small bits of sanity—tiny plump blueberries on a summer afternoon. They let me witness Truth as it was maddeningly unfurling before my eyes, and helped me see order in the chaos; they let me co-create the reality i craved most.

The seeds of this work were my healing task, to notice and document what we were enduring. That kept me present. The present moment i learned, was the only place i could serve my son.

***

Without these lush, literate meadows to write in, my thoughts, fears and hopes would have run feral, and i would have suffered far more than i did. Yet, it was not the mere unspooling of these words that enriched me, it was knowing, those late hospital nights, that they were being read. Thank you.

***

This is my account of what happened to us, and me in 2007 when my son fell from a tall tree. There are selected writings from my wife Tina and from members of our community, but the bulk of it is mine. As such, any foolishness, and all inanity i take full credit for. As to the rest, read it gently; may it serve you well.

ABOUT THIS BOOK

I wrote between bedside vigils in ICU, and after tucking the girls into bed at home when it was Tina's turn to spend the night at the hospital.

What comprises this book are updates that i published in real-time online or sent in emails to friends, plus words (like these) that i've written since. I've used as few words as possible for i value your time. As for lowercase *i*, i just prefer it.

> The real-time entries are set off from the main writing like this, indented, with a smaller font.

Folks grieved with us and for wounds unhealed in their own lives; they made us food and stood beside us in ICU. They added their lives to the story.

> *Their precious words are noted like this.*

***

Throughout the book, three small stars between sections are most closely intended as an invitation to pause, and perhaps breathe.

***

(Original Preface, Oct 2007) "I can count to 61!" Saskia announced. At four years of age, quite a milestone indeed!

I write this book because i have to. I write this book for Saskia, and for her eight year old sister Hanna, and of course for Felix, who fell out of a tree and started this whole daring adventure.

I write to my children for the time when they will be 19 years old remembering what happened that one crazy year, for when they turn

26 and are nurturing communities of their own, for when they are 37 and parents themselves.

I write so they can recall this amazing time, and so they can pass on stories to their children about what happened to our family that one summer long ago. I write too, to tell them i love them, more than i ever knew possible:

Dear Beautiful Hanna and Saskia and Felix, do not let your days pass without gratitude, without noticing the sublime beauty of Creation. To live is rare enough. To live and love, that is Divinity itself.

And please, never forget that i love you more than words could ever tell.

Yours, popi

ONE AFTERNOON

Nothing happens until something moves.

ALBERT EINSTEIN

JUNE 2, 2007, 2:35PM

"Mark!" came the panicked scream from a hundred yards across the lawn as soon as Saskia and i were within sight of the picnic area. It was Hanna's voice! Never before had i lived a sound so scared.

Red lights turned atop two ambulances where moments before a nine year old's birthday party had basked in the sunshine.

It had never occurred to any of us....

JUNE 2, 2007, 2:34PM

Before all this began we were living ordinary lives. My wife and i were raising three children, striving to find joy and meaning, breathing in and breathing out. We existed largely in 'this' world, the one of buildings and flowers, work and school and the riding of bikes. We lived in the world of bodies and growing older, desire and letting go—a world of trees and the climbing of trees.

There were certainly stirrings within our daily lives that this world wasn't everything there is to it. As we landed into middle age, the metaphysical questions what next? and why now? danced more often within our peripheral minds. We sensed, and were striving to find, the True Light that shines within each of us.

***

A few years earlier i had been introduced to yoga and meditation, and these ancient practices brought me incredible gifts: a spiritual approach to life and the seeking of Truth that i could direct from the inside out; a present-time physical practice that would be healthy for the rest of my days; and a large, growing fellowship of people i had something dearly in common with.

Yoga and meditation allowed me to perceive with calm much of the travail that came our way, and in those spacious moments i was able to see far.

I was blessed too, to be immersed in communities of diverse brilliance, but had no idea how vital this would be, nor how deeply i would draw from those precious wells in the months to come.

***

Tina and i had woven ourselves into hundreds of lives: at our children's schools, with the pre-natal yoga sisterhood Tina had nurtured, with our neighbors, Street Yoga, work colleagues and all the branches that grew outward from those limbs.

Portland is a small town wrapped in the guise of an almost big city. There seem to be no more than two degrees of separation between everyone in the Pacific Northwest. It was the perfect place for a young boy to fall from a very tall tree.

seconds before

beating within

his unremitting
stentorian heart
flooded everywhere
with life itself, as
the sun endows
all with
fire and warmth.

***

As in ancient days

cells begat new cells,
absorbed invaders and
transported energy
to broken friends
in need of reclamation.

They monitored change
and carried themselves
pulse by pulse
through
fluid and brawn.

***

Each cell lived
not alone
but in communion,

fellow cells
mingling
with entropy
while exchanging
transcoded
alchemical messages
inscribed
in the precise symbology
of weirdly folded proteins...

and all around,
synaptic responding
to electro-chemical
stimulation
played out
with quantum alacrity
along
sinewy
neural fibers
infiltrating the corpus
of his entire self.

All this every breath
and more,
so much more.

***

The next breath
spired ten million
exquisitely complex processes.

Beauty lived,

unnoticed by most
but observed fully
by gray matter,

realized by mind
and witnessed
by his soul
as God smiled upon,

activity
stillness
activity again.

What Mastery all this!

Breathe in...

Yes,

livers purge
while bones hold fast...

breathe out,

skins expel yet invite
only that which makes life
more firmly alive.

***

Look closer still,

the kidneys seem to decide
which molecules to keep,
and which to let go.

Whose Will is this?

Who decides
to linger the gaze,
or linger not
upon the upturned rose?

Is every living instant
a chance for each
to obey ancient dictates
or run amok...

to perform well
or not at all?

***

Consider,

what tiny spark animates
each speck of being?

Why did each cell
know so well
how to keep alive
the body
that held the soul,

and cherished the mind
of Felix Maus?

THE BOUGH BREAKS

Just keep breathing, Felix, and you'll be OK.
Please, just keep breathing.

AUTHOR, TO HIS SON, UNDER THE TREE

JUNE 2, 2007, 2:35PM

"Mark!" came the panicked scream from a hundred yards across the lawn as soon as Saskia and i were within sight of the picnic area. It *was* Hanna's voice; she had seen us. Red lights turned atop boxy ambulances parked beside the now-forgotten party.

Adrenaline cut with fear surged every cell in my body, and i grabbed Saskia's arm and ran her, half dragging, as fast as i could toward the terror in Hanna's scream.

Saskia and i had seen the ambulances moving along the edge of the park a few moments before, but had thought nothing of it. We had noticed, that is all.

It had never occurred to either of us that we'd find Felix broken on the hard ground, bleeding out on the bare roots of a now solemn cedar tree.

BENEATH

That Saturday started with the simple promise of sharing a fine spring afternoon in Portland with my three children: Felix, then age 10, Hanna 8, and Saskia 4. I love them more than words could ever tell.

Felix was a healthy, energetic, friendly boy who loved his family, adventuring, and playing the piano; Hanna was mature beyond her years, skilled at reading, writing, making flower bouquets, running a school for her younger sister, ballet and so much more; Saskia was an old soul, articulate and curious, a born orator, always using her words and wisdom to engage herself in the big wide world. Their mom, my dear wife Tina, usually had Saturdays for herself, and was visiting a friend and healer across town.

The kids and i set out on our bikes for Sunshine's birthday party at Laurelhurst Park a mile away. Sunshine was Hanna's friend, but we were all welcome.

Portland is a large small town, rich in diversity—conservative vegans living next to two-mom families who happen to like basketball and work closely with evangelicals in small high-rises downtown. People here relish building webs of connection that provide a special kind of wealth: mutual support, cooperative approaches to childcare, block parties, live neighborhood theater performances and lots of shopping at the countless local farmer's markets.

I had spent the night before at the Oregon coast sharing a rented house with a dozen parents from the coop preschool Saskia attended. We had enjoyed a late night together on the beach sipping wine around a huge bonfire, ostensibly planning the next year's activities, but more simply enjoying each other's company and growing close— we all knew we'd be caring for each others' children in the months to come, and it felt right to hear the sound of the waves together.

***

Looking back on my life in those days, what i will cherish above all else is the loving connection i felt with each of my children, the unique relationship we shared as they lived the first years of their lives.

Felix and i had been exploring the world together since he was days old, walking, busing, or biking around town. We loved nothing better than taking the #4 bus downtown, wander through hotels, office buildings or the university campus on our way to the farmer's market, stopping at the library or the candy store before heading back. I was home base for Felix, the safe return from any adventure. When i told bedtime stories, they always had lots of movement, sound, strength, and overcoming... heroic adventures that always ended in peace and clear resolution.

Hanna and i shared undying fondness for word, story and imagination. I knew the names of 20 of her 22 stuffed animals (sometimes confusing Benny and Tapiocapolis), and was always kept up to date on their challenges and triumphs. We held space together with a shared reverence for quiet, for sitting aside one another and reading our separate books, pausing frequently to update each other on the latest twists and turns. At bedtime, when stories were told, i always gave Hanna roles of extremely competent heroine, which she never failed to appreciate or live up to.

Saskia and i began conversing minutes after she was born. I would tell her of the larger mysteries during long walks when she was a few weeks old. Our exchanges grew into the two of us exploring the world together, discussing school teachers and best friends, sharing questions and poignant observations. She always wanted to know why, and would listen attentively when i explained the cellular differences between hair and skin, or the reason dogs don't talk like we do. At storytime, Saskia wanted harmony over adventure, resolution and balance over excitement, and i always cast her as the wise, far-seeing peacemaker, a nice grounding to her daring siblings.

***

That Saturday was one of the warm June days, humid and luxurious, green and sunny—the smells of nature so rich that even thirst and hunger were lessened by their organic fertility. We passed dozens of species of flowers on the short bike ride to the park, and half again as many conifers and broadleafs, radiant light greens mingling with purple-blacks as dark as tomorrow night.

Basking everywhere, vivid azaleas and bursting rhododendrons courted maidenly tulips, patient roses and impatient poppies as yellow Oregon grape called out to us along the way. It was a truly beautiful day, one of the sweet rewards Portlanders appreciate after long dark months of rainy gray.

At the park we found the party spread out over a broad glade anchored by the tall cedars of Picnic Area B. Felix was soon playing badminton, Hanna catching up with friends old and new. Saskia decided to wander off in search of something new. She didn't ask; she just started ambling downhill along the nearest path. I caught sight of her during one of my endless tri-kid visual sweeps, and after quickly ensuring that Felix and Hanna were fine, i hustled to join my youngest for a stroll in the park. I was tired, too little sleep, and roaming with my delightful four year old was something to relish.

The birthday party was like so many events in our lives during those years of raising young children in Portland, a unique assembly of friends and acquaintances from our many, often overlapping communities: school friends, co-workers, people we'd met at someone's solstice party or a friend of a friend who knew someone we didn't even know they knew.

Saskia and i passed a couple with a baby at peace on a blanket, and she stopped to tell them we were at the park for a party (and let them know their baby was cute). We ambled toward the duck pond five minutes away, and despite beckonings of cake and phone calls that i gladly ignored, we continued toward the water. Forty-eight hours later i wrote:

> we were at laurelhurst park for a party with one of hanna's friends (and dear sunshine and family, we are so sorry to have interrupted your birthday celebration). saskia and i were away at the duck pond, and felix and hanna were playing with the other friends. at some point, i heard my name screamed in a very frightening way; it was chilling, but i thought it was just shrieks from others in the park. there were two calls to my cell phone while we were feeding ducks, but not from a number i recognized and after a while, saskia and i made our way back to the party. we saw from a distance two paramedic trucks moving towards where we were going, so we decided to investigate on our way back.
>
> then we heard my name screamed again. it *was* hanna, and we started running, and arrived to find felix lying on the ground under a very tall tree, not moving. a bone was protruding from his wrist at a violent angle, his right thigh was bloody, his face was bruised, and blood was bleeding out his mouth, nose, ears and scalp. five paramedics surrounded him and were securing him to a backboard for immediate transport to the trauma center. he either wasn't breathing, or was breathing with incredible pain and dis-ease.

Slipping Away

Though i had tried to do no harm, Saskia still remembers the arm-wrenching pain of our run across the grass. I saw Hanna standing under the tree, a look of deepest fear on her face. I touched her briefly and moved quickly toward Felix. All the parents and children from the party were standing ashen-faced in a circle around us, numb at the witnessing of the nearness of death.

Felix Greene Lilly, ten years old, avid tree climber and lover of life, was not moving; he was broken and unconscious, and bones jutted out from his crushed right thigh and broken arm. He bled from his skull.

As i bent to his side i tried for the first of countless times to will him to survive. I told him gently that he had fallen, from a tall tree and was being cared for by paramedics, and that if he just kept breathing he would be OK.

Survival-time slowed as the hurrying dimmed and i noticed that we were somewhere very new but very old, kneeling on the ancient line between life and death.

> it is hard to describe the sheer terror of that time. it will live forever within me as the longest hour of my life.

That hour lasted 90 seconds and every journey, no matter the destination starts with a single breath. I had mine and all i could think was to plead with my son to keep drawing his. I knew with all my being that Felix's breath was on the verge of slipping away forever.

falling

armies of sentinel cells
knew within fragments
that danger had crossed
from possible to imminent.

Bear with.

Scout cells
ceaselessly patrolling
the edges of perception
registered minute vibrations
perturbed into being
by the whiplash
of cellulose
torn to splinters

as that one stout branch
heaved its final living breath.

***

Ripples in the mesh
were sensed—as alarm perhaps
or simply raw information
by neural constellations deep
in the young boy's ear

and from there
were hurled
along tympanic synapses
to agents alert
in his ever-vigilant brain.

Thundering cracks
fractured base equilibria
and rocketed stress
toward seats of discernment
to quicken,
and warn the rest
of his universe
that the threat to survival
had leapt
from near to now!

***

High above
the ground below
those blips
were the first gasp of horror
the Titanic's late-night helmsman drew
when he knew,
wholly and without doubt
that collision,
and catastrophe
were imminent.

Meanwhile,
the everyday cells
of this boy's symphony
were so well engaged
in the joyful creation
of abounding life
that pain, and gravity
were infinities away.

***

Meanwhile too,
riding pre-fall momentum,
flumes of exuberance
sluiced through organic tissue
to luxuriate small muscles
about his eyes

and cast down his gaze
from that sylvan perch
to see if anyone
was beholding his
keenly appropriate
schoolboy triumph.

***

Birds too, turned
to listen.

***

The billion-nanosecond splinter
traversed its inevitable surrender
to grave forces
alive within
earth's oldest core...

and ever more Felix-cells jumped
from joyful tasks
to a dread understanding
that death and its minions
were suddenly
close at hand.

CHOOSING

*Have patience with everything that remains unsolved
in your heart. Try to love the questions themselves,
like locked rooms and like books written in a foreign
language. Do not now look for the answers. They
cannot now be given to you because you could not
live them. It is a question of experiencing everything.
At present you need to live the question.*

RAINER MARIA RILKE, LETTERS TO A YOUNG POET

JUNE 2, 2007, 2:36PM

I recall being calm. I recall willing myself to keep moving, attending
to details, paying attention. I recall a sense of utter surrender to the
reality of right now, one of many glimpses in the days to come.

I felt neither prepared nor unprepared. My first awareness was
the need to witness everything, yet miss nothing. I had not overtly
readied myself for anything as grave as this.

Though i had practiced yoga for a number of years, and had spent
a lot of time through Street Yoga with young people dealing with traumatic crises, i felt ordinary. I was trying that summer to return to
freelance work, software and writing, and was two days from retiring
from a full-time job with benefits with a health insurer. I volunteered
every week and struggled to find my path in life just as i always had.
Most of all i was grateful for my family.

Under the tree, trying to absorb the impact of the fall on my being
as Felix's body absorbed the fall in his flesh, i found myself in a state
of wild stillness: quiet, alert, feeling fear but solid like the hard-
packed soil beneath us.

Yet, despite my complete, attentive desire to help my son, i knew of nothing that i could do! I couldn't insert a tube into Felix's airway; i couldn't staunch any unseen internal bleeding; i couldn't unscramble his pounded brain. All i could do was be present, answer the para-medic's questions and pray.

> hanna saw him fall. she was standing right there beneath the tree, and saw him plunge to earth.
>
> she and our friend fiona both recall that he landed on his right leg, which crushed the femur, then fell hard onto his right wrist, breaking that, before smashing his head on the ground, break-ing his skull in two places.
>
> damn! the poor dear boy. i write this to find some clarity amidst the sadness and some light amidst the chaos.
>
> felix was immediately attended by his sister and a number of attentive adults, who instantly knew to call 911. the paramedics were there very quickly. hanna and fiona both report that at this point they thought that felix was dead or dying, as he was not breathing, and was bleeding from his mouth, ears, nose, wrist, thigh and various other scrapes. he wasn't moving. it was about this time that i arrived to the panic and fear.
>
> what i first witnessed was felix on the ground surrounded by the paramedics, and everyone looking very grave. the night-mare was howling full force into me.

I knelt down at the left side of Felix's body. I tenderly touched his bloody head, told him he had fallen from a tree and that he was being cared for; i told him to hang tight and just keep breathing. Just keep breathing Felix, please.

***

Something old-school terrible had come our way to visit our family with its timeless pain; no matter what i had wanted minutes before, no matter my plans, this was now my life.

What confronted me in those plumbless first moments was the re-alization that i had to choose, fast. I had to choose how i would show up to this crisis, and i had to choose now!

Days later in one of those flash-moments, i remembered when i had been co-teaching a Street Yoga class to a group of teenage girls locked in a foster care shelter. The co-instructor told them: "I know you don't have a choice on whether to be here or not; but you do have a choice on how you're going to show up to our togetherness. That's entirely up to you!" Those words shot forward through time to meet me kneeling beneath the tree next to Felix. I chose, or these thoughts chose me:

- to notice everything without judgment.
- to be present, no matter how much it hurt, no matter how scary.
- to strive to accept what had befallen us without asking why me?
- to behold all that was happening in order to gain every possible advantage.
- to be completely honest; fabrications would detract from being present.
- to Love as much as i possibly could; when all else fails, Love.

All this transpired within a few breaths under the tree. I didn't etch these vows with a stick into the dry dirt next to Felix's crumpled body; it wasn't a logical effort.

It was an instantaneous knowing, a tacit agreement i made with myself that i would face this crisis with eyes, heart and soul wide open no matter what.

No matter what, i tried constantly to live up to that promise in the days to come.

***

None of this protected me from pain deeper than i had ever known, but as knowing jaggedly unfurled itself to my conscious awareness over the ensuing days, one sacred touchstone was revealed: the choices i made would matter. They had to! They would influence everything that lay ahead.

Choices inflect our lives, i saw, yet often ripen to influence only across years, and over strange calendars unseen by younger eyes. Under the tree everything was immediate, and every moment crucial.

Through years of yoga, meditation and earnest prayer, through uncountable stupidities and missteps, perhaps i had been preparing myself for this moment: how would i show up for my family when they needed me most?

WITHOUT JUDGMENT

Noticing came first. The act of mentally documenting everything my senses perceived took all my capabilities. I noticed what was going on around me, and what was going on within. Jiddu Krishnamurti once said "the highest form of human intelligence is to observe without judgment." Under the tree, i noticed:

- Felix was gravely injured.
- I was scared shitless that he was going to die.
- On his own, he could not breathe well enough to stay alive.
- Hanna and Saskia were not injured.
- A paramedic wanted to talk to me.
- Felix needed urgent trauma care.
- Hanna was ashen and trembling with fear.
- Friends would look after the girls.
- Felix might die at any moment.

The practice of noticing the world around me had its limits. Once all the details had been assimilated there was little else outside of myself to take in. After a full minute beside my son, he was still near death; i could not tell if we had inched closer or if we had crept back. My request to the paramedics to tell me the precise details of our future went unsatisfied. A gigantic chasm loomed within, around, and about me.

***

There was no turning away. No one could stand in for me in whatever was to come. I had to endure, as Felix's father, as father to Hanna and Saskia, as Tina's husband.

Everything i believed—about being a man and a father, every loving way i had shared with my children, every mindful practice i had ever learned to bring myself closer to the Truth—all were being thrown together and compressed into a tiny space no bigger than a single breath. What i felt was more vast than all i had experienced before, and to this i had to show up, come what may.

Every breath held the potential to deepen to despair if only i would allow it, if only i would give up and give in, yet i refused. There was simply no other choice as long as i had the power to choose, and to that power i held fast.

I had to show up for my son.

PROMISE OF THE PRESENT

During those first breaths under the tree, i noticed the exact position of Felix on the ground. I noticed the tilt of the sunlight in the afternoon sky. I felt ten years of joy and tears collapse into a single vision before me: i loved my children as Life itself.

The immensity of that moment was the starting point of my call to be present. I had to show up, above all else, to that sacred task. I had to love, as if my entire life depended on it.

Having chosen to notice, i found a deeper promise: i would dedicate my noticing to this moment alone. I would focus on what was occurring now and leave the future to reveal itself. This vow was made easier at first by the sheer volume of data there was to absorb, but i strived always to keep it throughout the flood in the weeks ahead.

From this, a second promise appeared: i would be present with full volition, even though none of this was on terms of my own choosing.

These two promises had a single shared purpose: to help keep my son alive, and our family whole. If i were ever to regret anything, it would be that i had failed to glimpse the one slim chance we might have had to survive. That, i could not abide.

***

Four paramedics worked to stop the blood and cerebrospinal fluid which was spilling from Felix's ears, mouth and nose. They splinted his bloody, mangled thigh and stabilized his jagged wrist, and put a cervical collar about his neck to protect his mind and future.

They worked calmly but hurriedly to ensure that Felix had an open airway, so they could squeeze oxygen into his voracious lungs. They strapped him to a board so they could safely transport him and his precarious spine to the trauma center.

One of the paramedics took me aside and asked if i were Felix's father. I said *yes*. He told me that Felix had fallen out of the tree, and had sustained serious injuries. Felix needed to be transported immediately to the Trauma Center at OHSU (Oregon Health Sciences University). I briefly checked in with my daughters, made sure they were going to be attended to, and then left with the paramedics for the ride up the hill.

***

With my son living or dying in the back of the ambulance, i knew i was standing face on to a silent earthquake.

> the ride was slow. i counted every car that failed to yield to our lights and sirens. i tried to see through the bodies in back diligently trying to get a breathing tube in, trying to get an IV started.

> we had to stop so that they could find the vein, and i felt very small, and very alone. there was no one to ride through this with me. even my wife, with the grief and fear i knew she would hold and be terrified by, would be merely another victim of this tragedy.

FIRST PRAYER

The ride to the hospital was scarcely bearable. We crawled. Speed bumps we took at 5 mph and every intersection was a swollen river to ford. Many cars raced through our crossing. The ambulance driver let up at every turn, announced every rise and dip and finally stopped under a freeway so the medics in back could safely plunge an IV into Felix's arm.

We sat beneath the traffic for two eternities while my son teetered on the brink of life and death, hope just a mile away up the hill. The ride had begun and i wasn't driving. I was holding on for dear life.

***

Prayer was a practice i had experimented with, but never earnestly; it had never been my living tissue. Now, seat-belted, the pulsing red light of the ambulance was my prayer, and prayer was my scoundrel's refuge.

I tried to kindle an ancient spark and let loose to a timeless universe tiny seaside-embers that were quickly engulfed by in-rushing waves.

I knew not where to send my pleas, only that i must make them—as a two year old must make noise—over and over again with all my force, through every possible means. I was seeking anyone, anywhere with the power to hear my heart and keep my son alive.

My praying that hour was wordy, imploring, without silence. Without silence, i became distracted from being present, and my head babbled in rambling discourse: *it was bad that Felix had fallen; was the tree to blame; was i?* Bad-ness became a magnet for memories of pain, loneliness and despair, and soon i was flooded with breath-taking terror. I was reliving moments that were moments old but they beat me blunt. My lungs recoiled from the blows.

I slowed my breathing in the brown vinyl ambulance seat, and struggled to return to my single purpose: keep Felix alive.

**

Opening to fear did not serve my son. If i were to catch the one forgiving straw in this raging hurricane i had to pay fullest attention every second, or i would miss once and for all time the narrow path of our survival.

The temptation to stray returned again and again... when the pain grew and the call to run and hide from the scarcely bearable grief was a siren's enticing lure.

In the ambulance, all i could barely do was remember to breathe.

ELEVATORS

Saturdays were sacred. We'd been adventuring in Portland since Felix was a wee lad 3 days old. I put him in the sling and we started walking. All over, and from there we eventually jumped on the bus, and got out of the house every Saturday early to go to the Farmer's market and the art museum, city hall and that big hotel near the office building with the magic glass elevator.

In the early years Tina simply needed a break after majority parenting all week. Hanna joined our family in mom's belly when Felix was 14 months, and Tina's need for Saturday morning rest expanded. After Hanna's birth, our adventures added the picking of fruit as a worthy part of a lovely day.

I've always craved solitude, yet with my children it was as if they were my flesh extended, so i could be alone with them and yet my soul was spacious, fully present and together.

EVERY PARENT'S NIGHTMARE

Still for the first time since the grave shadow had arrived, riding shotgun for a change, up hill—a hard half-hour after first contact—i realized we might die any second! *Good Lord No!*

He might have just passed away!! That might have been his last drawn breath.

Suffering happens in present tense.

**

The horrifying realization of death flooded in and filled me completely, a drenching i would endure again and again. Twisting in my seat i tried to see, strained to hear anything that might prepare me for the moment to come, for the cataclysm that i perceived so close. I tried, and failed, to read clues in the earnest body language of the paramedics.

The crazy blunt realism of those moments was the first nightmare come to life, the demon i had feared most since i laid eyes on my newborn son: *do not take my child before me.*

Primal cyclones of unstable emotion drove to scatter me into chaos; i breathed to survive. On the public computer that first night, in the hallway outside ICU i wrote:

> ...the nightmare was howling full force into me, every parent's worst nightmare, that any of us would lose a child.

> i longed to hold my dear boy, to put him together, but i was unable to be of service to him in any way but by simply being there with him.

Each breath was time travel through aspic moments: the contours of the inhale, a pause, the release of the exhale, another pause—all the while listening to the paramedics discuss details in the back, trying not to stay jacked on fear, praying they wouldn't tell the driver to slow down because it was too late, the siren going deaf as we eased into the final ride to the end of the line.

I cry as i write this.

And yet, it was more... so much more.

AT THE CHASM

JUNE 2, 2007, 3:29PM

Within seconds of docking at the Trauma Center, Felix was wheeled into the primary triage room. Specialists in white made a tight circle around his gurney.

Nancy, a soul-lovely social worker, attached herself to me. That was her job; i was 'dad', my title and my role. The other staff had different tasks, like keeping death at bay, and "*dad!*" was guaranteed to get me out of the way fast.

Twenty well-trained folk—brain people, bone people, heart, surgery and blood people were packed three deep around Felix. On call, they had raced from all over the hospital to save a young boy's life. I tried to look through their bodies to see my son.

I strained yet again to hear meaning from the calm frenzy of medical voices, but found no answers. I stood as tall as i could, and Nancy shadowed me, and i was grateful. I knew that if doctors came to tell me that Felix had died, she would be right there to absorb the first flood of my eternal grief. Moments in, because i was cold, she gave me a maroon long-sleeve flannel shirt.

ELEVEN MINUTES LATER

A white male doctor emerged from the triage scrum. He told me Felix was severely injured and they were doing everything they could. He needed an immediate CT scan to determine if his brain was too swollen to fit inside his skull without bulging out the bottom. If so, a surgeon would immediately remove a part of Felix's skull temporarily so his brain could swell with less peril to primary survival.

I consented to all this in an instant and Felix was wheeled by, too fast to touch. He was pushed down a hall, through two broad white doors through which i could not pass, like Clockwork Orange. The doors hissed slowly closed and i stood still and faced the barren landscape before me.

***

I knew he might die. That was a plausible outcome to his injuries. That thought made me very sad. Nancy stood close. Twenty minutes passed.

She was tuned to my being. If i were to collapse in fear, she had a protocol for that. If i started screaming because despair overcame all resistance, instinct and experience would inform her what to do. She was good. She reassured me, as only few could right then.

I stood, feet parallel, about hip distance apart.

With partial witness, i tried to balance from front to back and side to side. Whatever was going to happen, i needed to be fully present, fully awake to take it in.

Once or twice, i remembered to breathe.

***

In the hazy aftermath days later i wrote...

> when we got to OHSU, the trauma team was ready, like actors on their marks before the curtain rises.

> they wheeled him into the first triage room, and two social workers began to shadow me. nancy wouldn't leave my side, and her aide would get me water when i asked.

after a few minutes of craning into the packed room, seeing nothing, straining to hear 'oh shit, we're losing him' or 'get the crash cart' or 'come on buddy, don't die on us now...'

a doctor came and told me Felix was severely injured and they were doing everything they could. he had a massive brain injury, and multiple compound fractures.

That first doctor made no promises. He would not assure me that Felix would survive the next ten minutes. I was alone. I could not deflect the penetrating glare of death's lightless gaze. But—breathe out, Felix lived.

Breathe in, behold, Felix's death as i stared at it waiting was horrific... no demons or smoke. Rather, it was the complete absence of everything that i know from *this* life.

There was no light, no smell, no taste, no hope—no fear dreams or tomorrow, no noise breath or blood. There was no companionship left, no future, no us, no soul just *nothing*!! The Story was ended. Felix's death through my eyes was a vacuum so great that i could not possibly imagine surviving its endless reach.

i was made to stand at the side of a huge chasm of blackness. it was an endless fall of 'absence'. it was death. one step forward, one word or grim look from the doctors and i would be forced to step into the emptiness, never to fully return again.

it was the longest quarter hour of my life. there was nowhere to run to, nowhere to hide. any prayer that came to my lips seemed small compared to the vastness of death, i simply stood there feeling the icy wisps swirl around me.

I stood at the edge. It was a small edge, about a foot deep. I could not step back while Felix was being scanned. I had no desire to step forward into the void, off the highest cliff i had ever beheld.

SHOTS FIRED LONG AGO

Since i was 18, i have always felt death near. That summer i worked as a teller in an air-conditioned branch of a savings and loan bank in the San Fernando Valley of Los Angeles, North Hollywood, California.

One morning, four black men burst into our bank over my right shoulder and after yelling for *all us motherfuckers to get on the floor and give them all our money!* one of them ran up to me and shoved two handguns straight into my unbroken face.

He—about 26 and convinced that robbing me to the edge of death was a good idea—pushed a bag across the counter and demanded that i give him all the bills in my teller drawer. He vaulted over, pushed the guns into my back and walked me down the line as i stuffed the bank's cash into his satchel.

As i emptied the last till, i dropped under the counter, freaked and flinched as one of the robbers fired his gun right past the head of the old lady running the vault. The other robbers responded instantly with gunfire of their own and bullets ricocheted all throughout the confines of that small, commercial space.

And just as quickly, they were gone.

***

I was wrecked. I couldn't deal, didn't know that dealing well was a good idea, and a few weeks later, early September, i left my childhood behind for university 400 miles north.

In my new home, i didn't handle the trauma at all. I had no sense that almost getting one's head blown into a thousand irretrievable pieces was an event that could take hold.

I got high with Kevin seconds after parking my car that first Berkeley moment, probably five years to the day before he took his own head off with a shotgun. Rest in peace bro, and find your Truth.

***

For ten years, I buried the fears that grabbed me too often. I ran, denied, pretended, medicated myself and for my efforts, night terrors, weak relationships, constant insecurity and an easily startled, hyper-vigilant nature.

In many ways it was a lost time, but i did learn a lot about fear, and about myself.

***

The pain i felt decades later—not knowing if my son was alive or dead —was dread of a different blood, not the adrenaline fear of the bank robbery, but the ancient misery of a parent watching their child bleed toward death.

Twice afraid in my life, really afraid, and powerless both times to do anything but endure.

BEARING WITNESS

Waiting in the Trauma Center for the blank doors to open, prayer seemed insignificant. I looked down at my feet and wondered how could i, in my insignificance, deign to speak into the emptiness on my son's behalf? To whom could i offer up my own life in exchange for his?

Death happens, even to 10 year old boys. Mistakes are made, life ends at some point and what special favors did i deserve?

I prayed, though. Humbly, silently, earnestly. I was quiet. I stood, and beheld the vast emptiness before me.

***

I felt powerless to alter the outcome, so i existed and tried to notice. My yearning did not budge the situation one parsec. Felix had his journey to make, and i had mine.

I didn't know where he needed to go, where he was destined to travel, so i had to serve as fully as possible while i still had the chance. I found a waiting area and sat.

There were no windows to the outside and the room was shaped like a weird polygon from 8th grade math. It had armchairs and a two person couch, functional end tables and indirect lighting. Between prayers and silence i imagined 'the conversation' with the doc.

I saw myself standing there when the same physician would approach. He would ask me to sit, but i would know instantly. I would know my life sentence long before it was ever handed down.

I heard in my imaginings his tone of voice and tried on the words he would say; i saw him rehearsing the dreaded moment—hating this part of being a doctor, the bearing of news that would shatter a family forever.

Then i chose to stop imagining and stood tall with what i believed was real. I did not know what was coming our way; far better to watch it arrive than sit in fantasy with what might never be.

> i breathed. i stood. i felt my place in the universe and at that moment, there was nothing else.

> the doctor came... this was my time. i was being called to the tipping point to hear my fate.

> felix was severely injured, he said, but there was no sign of such excessive swelling that would require emergency brain surgery.

he was being transferred to the intensive care unit where he would be given the best care for his many injuries.

Everything was present tense! Felix lived!! I trembled through. A dense, bone-hugging garment fell from my body and i was naked. I stepped back from the edge, sentence commuted; for now, a mere 90 minutes had passed since Felix fell, and yet i had aged a dozen years.

Felix and i had played badminton together a few heartbeats before, rolled hoops down the hill and chatted with friends old and new.

Had we been hiking when the branch broke in a rural community without rapid response, had we been traveling, had the paramedics been delayed by another tragedy or had he landed an inch or two this way or that and ripped a cerebral artery, Felix would have died right there under the tree. Of that i am certain.

***

Felix and his team went one way to the Pediatric Intensive Care Unit (PICU), and i was escorted by Nancy to the picu waiting area, ninety yards from my son's new room. As she moved off, i imagine she exhaled and prepared herself for the trauma to come. I never saw her again; she birthed me into the hospital and i still wear the maroon shirt she shared to keep me warm.

To bear witness is to observe—with compassion and without judgment—what is truly going on. Telling a story illuminates darkness, for oneself and others, and a few days later i began to tell ours...

Mon, JUNE 04, 2007 09:48 AM (first online journal entry)

Felix fell from a tree in Laurelhurst Park on Saturday, June 2nd. He sustained serious injuries and is in the pediatric intensive care unit at Doernbecher Hospital in Portland.

I awaited Tina's arrival outside the ICU, and the moment they would let us in to see our injured son.

mid air

as the last wood fibers gave way,

primal deciding woke
from sanguine quiescence
and directed him to act,

his lungs inhaled sharply
and forests of adrenaline
slammed his body
with uncut speed...

he screamed—

air yelling across taut vocal cords as
arms flailed at ghostly currents
of unknown vibration
that keened in the
oddly still
green June air.

***

Muscles exploded
and fired again
to keep his head
from hitting first,

but fingers found no purchase
in the suddenly thin
near-earth
atmosphere.

Impact drew close
and one thought,
one thought alone:
protect the brain!

***

Right foot crashed
at speed unsustainable
to all integrity
and crumbled,

and in that first half beat
memorizing stopped
as all nerves were commandeered
for only those purposes
that promised
the chance
at mere survival.

Pressure surged
in upper leg
until a single meme
directed
all organs
to flood his entire body
with clarity and sedation
everywhere
at once.

Brain witnessing was bypassed
so he wouldn't react wrong
and get fatally
in his own way.

***

Force,

hundreds of pounds
per square dot,
raged across
a six millisecond
impact wave,

seismic lines
shuddering bone, hip
and hard ground
alike resisting,

yet refusing to yield
until physics
demanded
that
all
energy
be fulfilled.

***

His femur imploded
with violent surge
and shattered muscle, fat and skin
as the echo
disturbed a butterfly
half a mile from the
sudden, unexpected pain.

His body continued its collision
with mother earth,
while his mind fended off
a frantic chorus
of threats beyond experience.

In garbled bursts
immune sub-systems
were yelled at
by an overwhelmed brain
to produce new cells
of every kind
at ten thousand times the normal rate
and rush them
to every point of injury
everywhere
at once!

***

His wrist blew apart
and burst out through skin
as gravity's thirst
began to slake...

but enough power remained
to pull Felix's head
into the ground
at what must have been
27 solid miles per hour...

forty feet per second

his brain
careened to a halt
while his skull bounced
and all was quiet
under the tall tree in the
oddly still
green June air.

CIRCLE OF LOVE

Never Despair!

PIERRE DERAVIGNAN

JUNE 2, 2007, 4:45PM

When Tina arrived at the waiting lounge outside the PICU, we held each other, looked into each others' fractured faces, then retreated again to our own private torment.

It was unexpected, i remember thinking, that we could be of so little comfort to each other. We were in such extreme shock that caregiving another was out of the question. We had neither the strength nor the wisdom to share hope with anyone. We co-endured the nightmare.

A powerful chill swept us bare. We were first steps into a journey as ancient as tree-covered hills that used to be mountains.

Tina and i were scared, and took chairs beside each other, both unreachable in our own grief.

***

For five hours we sat, ate, drank water and stared into the well-meaning orange walls of the waiting lounge. We were ICU periphery, away from the medical hubbub but deep inside the dark shell of a parent's grief.

I appreciated the odd cleanliness and ragged order of that room... toys stacked in corners, toys shoved between the cushions of our comfortable chairs, toys last touched by hands as shocked as we were to be there—or oblivious; there was that.

We used the phone. We sat, stood, sat. We talked quietly. We wondered, as questions died on our lips, if Felix were still alive. We waited for permission to continue living out the details of those lives we'd once called our own—lives we had blood-shared with our children since first inspiration.

I remember feeling ashamed to eat. It was one floor up, across the skywalk and six floors down to fetch a dry tempeh wrap with carrot slivers and coffee. What right did i have to live well!? Calling family was subdued and grave, conversations brief, each loved one absorbing the blow to their own extended lives.

Two doctors apprised us of their assessment. Their words, beyond telling us that Felix was alive, were a blur.

We called Hanna and Saskia by phone. They were watching Kiki's Delivery Service at Jane and John's. They both asked about Felix, then Saskia told us about the characters in the movie, and Hanna asked more about her brother. She didn't speak much, but reassured us that all was well there with her and her sister.

We rang off; they were having popcorn, but Hanna was shaken, i could tell through the phone. Then back to worrying about her brother with full focus of my willable, attentive being.

*****

Finally a nurse came and told us that Felix was stable (read 'alive') but severely injured, and we could see him now. She said they were doing the best they could for him. We did not ask about the future.

We followed her to ICU room 13 and found our son lying on an inclined hospital bed, a dozen tubes weaving in and out of his young, battered body.

We moved to his side, touched him, felt his warm living energy and told him we loved him more than we had ever realized before.

*****

We hurt so deep... his right eye was swollen shut, and blood and spinal fluid leaked out of ears, nostrils and his once talkative mouth. His pulse raced and limbs were streaked with red.

Sensations, reflexes and emotions, fragments of thoughts and shards of memories all erupted within and shot through me. I was unbidden, copious with fear, quick to tears and grateful purely that we were still alive. Confusion, calm and anxiety flung themselves at me from primal places of near-despair, despair i worked hard to keep at bay.

That was the first task of parenting in ICU: never despair. Yank it out by roots and be done. Despair was poison, craving to engulf me and choke away any possibility of being present with my son.

Bedside, ICU

Seven hours in and we longed for relief, but found tangled chaos instead. Clearing apart the stimuli was clawing through thistle and scabs, while monitors streamed incessant numbers of colored fear and wove stories we longed never to hear.

One set of right-moving blips recorded the dynamics of his still beating heart, tangible proof that life still lived in Felix Maus. Tubes infused, lines drained and wounds bled as swelling grew.

Smell arrived from all direction—flesh smells, medicine-sweat and urine smells. Antiseptic odors seeped in from beyond our door—fear smells, death and life smells. The waste sucked from his stomach was brown, and told of swallowed dirt and bleeding within.

The skin around his eyes darkened as blood seeped from busted capillaries, and bandages under his nose soaked up twin streams of clear and red, gauze squares that would be swapped out every few minutes for days to come. The rate of vital fluid seepage became another barometer to track, another commitment to notice—yet one more particular quality of Felix's continued existence to appreciate while we still had the chance.

Each such pledge carried a mountain of heartache if he died.

***

The full catalog of his injuries was not beyond counting, yet i was stunned. The nurse had been with Felix for hours when we were allowed in and still she worked without pause, adding fluids to his IV's, emptying his urine bag, suctioning his lungs, swapping bloody gauze for dry, checking vital signs on the monitors overhead—fingers, eyes, mind working, assessing medical needs that she could address, and the ones she would defer to others. Some she probably abandoned forever.

We were shocked at his tidied, mangled flesh.

Our immediate task, the only one that seemed attainable, was to send out waves of Love to Felix as strong and as hardy as any we had ever mustered before.

***

In the same breath, we had to respond to the fact that he was utterly unresponsive, totally unmoving and oblivious (as far as we could tell) to everything. He seemed to be sinking deeper into coma's soothing sleep, giving in to the seduction of the narcotics and maybe even entertaining the lure of death... all before our watchful, pleading gaze.

We touched what unbloodied spots on his head we could find and whispered our love. We watched; fear was close.

I was not under direct threat. I was physically untouched. There was no form or thing to fight against, nothing to flee. What remained was choice: check out or stay present. It had to be faced—serve my son, serve my son, or serve something else entirely, something i wanted far away and gone.

Fleeing in any capacity would have left Felix without my strength, no way for me to help him survive, to survive and hopefully recover.

> only by staying present was i able to make it through. and only by staying present was i able to know at each moment what i could do that was best for felix. i cared for nothing else. i had no other task.

I could never have forgiven myself if i had abandoned him at his time of greatest need.

***

I watched the machines above the bed, felt his skin, touched his face. I studied the nurse's expression and perceived the scent of injury and disinfection, seeking at first glance what to do next.

Scant clues were forthcoming. Adrenaline prevented sleep and my exhaustion grew.

I needed to pee, to drink water, but somehow it felt disrespectful to allow myself those healthy body functions in the face of this calamity. I had an instinctive need to feel his pain, in the vain hope that it would ease his suffering. I wanted to transfer his injuries to my body by ethereal osmosis.

Time passed without the passing of time. We were in a world of continual activity where the lights would never go out and the life-meaning beeps would only fall silent when we departed ICU, one way or the other.

Now

The bumpy turbulence of the scene before me amplified turmoil within. I would have to pass through this asteroid belt as best i could. There would be no rescue, no resetting our lives to the way it used to be.

I felt full-body that the only way to survive was live one moment at a time, each moment full immersion, and deal with the next the instant it came. So as to not get overwhelmed, i broke each moment into smaller chunks, and aligned the rhythm of my steps with the flow of my breathing. My thoughts jumped.

The surest way to measure the length of one moment, i decided, was the breath. I tried to watch myself breathe and i tried to breathe slow.

One breath equaled one moment. I would limit all thought, all feeling to this breath's moment alone. If i did, there would be cosmic hints, attention-power freed up, power i could devote to noticing where best to serve my son.

Later

Around midnight that first night, in the hallway outside Felix's room Tina began to shake and shudder, and cry out that she couldn't take it anymore. She was near complete melt-down.

"This can't be happening!" she pleaded, her voice rising toward a wail. Her soul-walls were caving in right there under the deep fluorescents.

She began to crumble toward the floor, muscles giving in to general strike and i grabbed her and held her up against the massive pull of gravity.

> i held her very strong and told her in a fatherly voice that she had to choose who to serve at that moment—herself or felix.

> it was a stark and brutal choice, but if she broke down and needed me, neither of us could care for felix.

I would have abandoned her right there on the floor of ICU, of that i am certain. If she had truly lost her power, i would have returned to Felix's bedside alone and left her to others.

To her great, undying credit, she breathed deep and found within the Mother's Core that had cried out in such pain years before when this same injured boy was bloody-born.

She rose, and went back to that place of ultimate endurance and came to stand next to her possibly dying son.

SIMPLE

Tina was mothering Felix already, a few hours into our new life, fully unnoticed by me. She didn't announce it and it was days before i caught on and appreciated what she did by love and primal instinct alone.

She rubbed his feet, mopped his brow, held his hand, cleaned his face, kissed his forehead and whispered to him her Love. It was her best grounding.

Sometime during those first hours, Felix's nurse told us their job in ICU was to keep Felix alive by supporting his biological functions so that he could heal himself.

That was our first tangible clue as to what we, Felix's devoted, longing parents were supposed to do. We were there to help Felix heal. They kept him alive; we helped him get better.

That belief became the simple, central core of our work in ICU, and the first splash of solid ground we would have for days to come. It took months to understand the power implicit in that directive, but in ICU, it was a few cc's of oxygen within a grave and suffocating night-mare.

DEVOTIONAL WATCHING

We would have stayed at Felix's bedside for eternity if we could have physically endured, but the pull of flesh was inexorable and we could not maintain our vigil without rest. Our shared mortal fragility had never been clearer.

Yet one more thing to accept: we would have to let our eyes close and potentially miss the most crucial seconds of our entire lives. Rest well, son.

To accept is to stare Truth in the face and not pretend it's anything but. We had to accept that our son might die before dawn. We had to accept that there was precious little we could do to stop it.

***

Somewhere in those hours another need arose, the need to connect with people outside our injured family. I wanted to share and be heard, to be comforted and reassured, to find that someone, somewhere cared about our plight, and maybe knew a way out. I longed for a secret miracle.

Sometime that first night i wrote a friend i had been sitting with on the beach 24 hours before and sent her the first words of this tale.

> hi Susan, just wanted to connect with you tonight. felix fell about 25 feet out of a tree today at laurelhurst park and was knocked unconscious. he suffered a compound fracture of the femur, of the wrist, two skull fractures and a small fracture of the neck. he is currently in intensive care at OHSU where he will spend the night....
>
> i have no request attached to this other than that you might send a prayer felix's way. he's such a dear and loving boy and he is so battered tonight, it breaks my heart.
>
> we have all logistics covered. hanna and saskia are staying w/ friends and the rest of our matters are in hand. god willing, the worst is over and we're into recovery and recuperation. we'll spend a long night at his bedside tonight and pray we will greet tomorrow with good news about our son.
>
> blessings to you,
>
> love, m

Already, i was trying to build a new reality, an earnest world where rejuvenation was certain, and healing walked just over the horizon.

***

Years later, age 13, Hanna wrote:

> Everyone has nightmares. If it be about spiders or robbers, death or destruction, they still make your skin crawl and your breath quicken. But never in a million years do you think your nightmares will come true.

I never thought so. However, fate weaves its silken tendrils into our lives, sending all sorts of things to keep us on our toes.

It was bright and sunny the day my nightmare came true.

***

Around 2am, we surrendered to the nurse's urging to rest and slowly made our way to crooked repose. Tina stretched out on the six-foot window bed, and i on the large, padded chair. We tried to encircle Felix in our Love as we slipped toward broken sleep. We prayed that the most difficult part was over; we prayed silently, as our eyelids closed without our consent.

broken

inside

there must have been stillness...
if only for an instant,
so that all could sip
at least once from
the solitude of obliteration.

***

Was there
in that timeless
quantum oscillation
a silence,
stunned or otherwise?

Was there a witnessing
within each cell
of the enormity of all creation,

a microscopic gazing
supine
through starry night sky
to infinity and beyond?

Did each cell
hold sharp awareness
that it was part of something
profoundly vast,
yet beyond comprehension?

***

With perception so sweetly tuned
understanding came quickly...

and then to work,
order and duty
encroaching upon pandemonium,
battle joined again.

First responder cells shook off terror
and hurried
through tunnels packed
with staggering refugees
escaping undreamed of
calamity.

Body heaved and mind recoiled
in a cascading triage
of system-wide
recalibration.

Blood flooded veins
at once too fast
and too slow,

jetsam bashing glucose
as armed killer cells elbowed
for tube-space and
transports capsized in
channels clogged
with elements
ripped loose
from molecules
that used to work,

but now lay broken
dying
dead.

WE COME TO ICU

I've been siftin' through the layers
Of dusty books and faded papers
They tell a story I used to know
And it was one that happened so long ago

It's gone away in yesterday
Now I find myself on the mountainside
Where the rivers change direction
Across the Great Divide

KATE WOLF, ACROSS THE GREAT DIVIDE

JUNE 3-4 | DAYS 2 & 3

I woke 4:11am Sunday with a quick start to the monitors, and knew by their undiluted hum that Felix still lived. Thirty-four seconds of consciousness and everything appeared as it had been 96 minutes before. By daybreak our most earnest prayers remained unanswered.

WHAT I MISSED

Part of me perceived what Hanna had lived through at the park: witnessing Felix fall, seeing him grasp at mere air a slice before hearing the actual snap of the branch. She was there, first to absorb the impact of death's sudden arrival. She saw the scream, and has nightmares still. She continued:

> If man were gifted with the helpful sight of the future, I would have begged my brother to stay on the ground.

> From my vantage point on the ground, I saw just how high up in the tree my brother was.

> I advised him to come down, but he did not heed my warning. Mere seconds later I heard the crack, magnified a thousand-fold, echo through my head. Some people say that when devastating or destructive things occur, time slows. It was not so for me. Felix fell fast. Too fast. Then came the impact, leaving him bruised, bloody and seemingly dead.
>
> Screams pierced the air, mine joining the terrible orchestra, rising like a dove above the rest.

She was by his side while parents frantically dialed 911 to report a grave and urgent threat, and she was with him as he ebbed in the near between, watching flesh drain away into dusty soil.

As he lay dying, Hanna understood what she was seeing. She was just old enough to know that some stories aren't made up, and big brothers don't always live forever.

I imagined him through her eyes... Felix in the dirt—wounds hot, messy decay quickening. He was jagged everywhere and couldn't stand because his femur had just exploded through his leg, couldn't talk because his skull was cracked and he couldn't sit up because his wrist was destroyed.

Our minds absorb only so fast, and i felt in a vague and wordless place her powerlessness beneath the tree. She wrote:

> I could practically see his life mingle with the dirty roots of the tree, on the verge of slipping away forever. When the paramedics arrived I was hidden away in a grove of trees. I can still remember the graffiti carved into the smooth bark. I emerged only to ask a single question: "Is he going to die?"
>
> What a job that must be, having to answer that question with as much truth as possible. The woman looked at me with sad eyes and said "We're doing everything we can to keep him alive."

Come In

Arriving ICU took time. I had to learn how to rest, to eat and where to find water. I had to find circles of trust and where the exits were. I had to adjust everything and exist only in the present.

Meanwhile, my soul lived everywhere, trying to catch up and praying this insanity would stop immediately.

Sleep was half-conscious tossing beneath un-dimmed lights as resident ICU machines droned, raised alert and went about their un-sentient lives.

Every few injured minutes Felix's body misfired, alarms rang and my mind shot open as my body jerked and my eyes tried to remember where in God's name we were. My soul asked if the end had come.

***

The nurse quieted the dark noise, tuned sensitivities and told me i could go back to sleep. Sure, just wake me when death comes roaring back again.

The Intensive Care Unit is the last stop. The goal is to survive, and you either get better or you die. They don't tell you that when you walk through the doors, but you pick it up pretty quick. There's nowhere else to go.

hushed

but not quiet

entire hemaducts
were wiped away.

Engineer cells
determined
ceaselessly
to bypass destruction
and restore
precious movement
to tributaries
that had once nourished
every province
of his mortal being... and

in that instance before
lungs remembered
to breathe again,
teams swelled damage zones
and dispatched reports
at all speed
toward the brain,

Send help!

Send power and liquid,
blood cells, t-cells and specialists.

Raw materials and proteins are scarce
and comfort's been put to work!

***

Animated neurons
assessed electro-pulses
and drew forth
from deep reserves of
human knowledge
inchoate bits
that perhaps
held the secret
to everything that lives.

His ancient brain
assimilated messages
and directed action.

Cells on the skin assembled
at pre-ordained sites
and held forth
against intruders;

they forwarded a common plea:
we're being attacked,
come quickly!

***

The vast divide
that had long separated
inside from out
was burst wide open,
and swarms of bacteria
flooded up from soil,
down from sky
and in from platoons
that had since birth
been ceaselessly scouting
his skin for the
smallest crack.

Flesh tore and
single-cell life
poured in,

invaders bent
on devouring
blood-rich tissue
and colonizing
progeny deep
into the vital organs
of a suddenly
small boy
under
a very tall tree.

Unless his body capitulated first,
or overcame.

***

The demand was beyond precedent,
and oxygen was running short.

HOME

Don't turn away.

*Keep your gaze
on the bandaged place.*

*That is where
the light enters you.*

RUMI

DAWN SUNDAY | DAY 2

Sixteen hours in, i still thought we would patch up the hurt and be home by Wednesday. We were scheduled to be moved to a different hospital across town where orthopedists would repair his limbs, and late morning the transport team arrived, all sporting the bright red apparel that identified them wherever in the hospital they went.

They moved Felix's tubing from stationary to rolling stock and transferred his wires from fixed to portable. It was a full hour of fuss-ing before a side comment of mine about insurance threw pause into the action; staff gladdened, for our family retained extended coverage from my old job—generous insurance that was right and true.

Non-medical consultations were held, and it was determined we could stay; orthopedists would be found. We re-arrived, reconnected, returned to the same bedside room, ICU-13. Nothing had changed, except we were older.

***

The rest of the day was a blur about which i kept few notes. I felt dirty, shabby, unkempt. At some point i went home with a list: phone charger, clean underwear, toothbrushes, toothpaste, insurance info, cash, sweaters. Tina had scarcely left Felix's side. I must have checked-in with the girls at Jane and John's while gathering supplies, but i don't recall. It seems like i would have. Little of that second wave made it to long-term memory. I returned to ICU, and sat at Felix's bedside.

I stared at him, prayed, stood. I studied the monitors, mopped his forehead, breathed. Pray, stare, mop, sit, watch, stand, repeat, repeat, repeat. Breathe. Check the clock, five minutes. Grow restless, bored, then feel guilty. Seek escape, if only temporary, not really abandoning my post but scouting the vital terrain.

Keeping uninterrupted vigil was too compressed for me to handle well.

***

I walked, found exits just in case, and marked the ICU—24 single rooms about a central helm. I was a voyeur into other peoples' nightmares, and many times i would pass an empty room and feel the heavy spirits that lingered, only to find the next filled with a weeping, frightened family standing around a tiny, plexiglass bassinet.

I know how you feel, i wanted to shout!!!

It's nuts to be here, isn't it?!?!?! They would understand. Who else knew how crazy it was to hold death at bay in ICU.

***

You don't stay in ICU, at least i didn't. I lived there. My family's center of gravity had shifted irrevocably uphill, splintered, and taken a precipitous dive toward shallows far below. I resisted centrifugal acceleration and found myself already at home in our small corner of the big city hospital.

I couldn't talk to other denizens of ICU. What if...? What if their kid had just died? What if they were going home and we weren't?

Better to walk in silence, stay out of the way and wonder. In the ICU, to paraphrase one of the docs: bad things happen fast; good things always take time.

Intensive Care is a whole-body place, where every mood touched every sense and smells raced faster than i could track, moved along by quiet human steps and hvac acceleration.

Demeanor shifted with incisive cuts and acuity rose, fell and careened, as conversation grew muted or lively depending on who was living or dying in any given instant.

There's time, and ICU-time. In ICU-time, seconds last a lifetime and months fit onto the tip of a poised hypodermic syringe.

***

On a bulletin board outside the efficient ICU kitchen, hand-made cards thanked staff for heroic effort, while solemn ones announced funerals for children who had died too soon. Nurses flinched, and knew that a child's death is always too soon, and dozens of small containers of cranberry juice waited patiently on neatly labeled shelves.

Some families never leave ICU alive, and back in his room it was clear that Felix wouldn't have survived without masterful intervention. One by one, the ICU staff had moved responsibility for his bodily functions to machines, and substituted devices for organic activity.

Breathing became the ventilator's role. Urine drained from his bladder by catheter to a bag hanging from his bed-frame, and fluid volumes were stabilized by intravenous plasma as liquids were leached measure for measure into his needy veins.

Attentive caregiving was constant. God bless. Electrolytes irrigated blood and brain while opportunistic infections were battled by a steady barrage of ever-shifting antibiotics. His miraculous heart, though, kept beating all on its own.

Soon enough we would have to face a wide range of troubling questions, but for that afternoon each cardiac pulse was cause for celebration.

***

Late Sunday our dear friend Melody showed up from nowhere. She had heard. I greeted her at the entry to ICU and told her Tina could use support. She knew exactly what that meant, having spent the summer before in Intensive Care with her father-in-law recovering from an accident of his own. She stayed a long time then left, to the quiet, other night.

Tina and i settled bedside once again.

Downhill where we had lived days before, Jane and John sheltered the girls, Jeremy and Deah setup a Caring Bridge website, and

Karin and Jeff looked after our house. People emerged from the throes of their busy lives to help us keep ours.

I knew that if i had broken that night, i could have called and a dozen people would have come to the hospital at once. That humble, powerful truth was not thought, but was felt as a weary traveller might lean against a sturdy, middle-age oak; it was filed away, information from yet another source, real plus potential energy at our disposal whenever we needed.

I held a full quiver, and my heart rejoiced.

***

I didn't call anyone for help that Sunday night. I knew not what to ask for and so i endured, blind to alternatives.

TRUE ARRIVING

Arriving is a practice. It spans minutes, centimeters and discrete observations. Under the tree, i was forced to arrive within a single breath.

In ICU it took 48 hours to land, the first 24 devoted to being stunned, the next 24 to the heavy work of accepting that we needed intensive care and would be here for a long time.

Sunday night was less eventful than the first. I caught a few hours of chair sleep, and woke hoping the previous day's lack of bad news would continue.

***

Monday first light we learned that Felix's hematocrit was so low they decided to give him more plasma: too few red blood cells circulated to provide enough oxygen to his tissues or his brain. To my mind that wasn't supposed to happen; every intervention meant something wasn't working as it had 42 hours before.

There were more hospital personnel present than there had been over the weekend: more doctors, more students, more nurses, more therapists. It was their workday.

Monday early brought rounds—doctors stopping by to gawk and consult. The surgeons discussed doing a CT scan of his abdomen to see if internal injury could be spotted; if so, surgery would be performed and the bleed fixed. Two orthopedists arrived, senior and junior. They talked with us about Felix's surgery, when he would be stable enough to allow them to operate and repair his arm and leg. They were confident of their success.

Then the neurosurgeons came and layered grim over everything.

NEAR DEATH

The doctors we had encountered so far had spoken cautiously, seeking balance, striving not to create false hope but offering space for something less than dire possibility. The senior brain surgeon had none of that.

He emphasized at once the worst case: 'life-threatening', 'near-death', 'brain-dead'. The words hammered me down. I wrote out my fear and frustration:

> we know we are in a critical situation, but we had come to believe that we were at least one step removed from death's door. the news has been good—or rather, lacking much bad news— but this morning was a heavy weight to bear.

Every doctor had different experience to draw from. That made it harder; they weren't making stuff up. The surgery people spoke fluently of using skill to stop bleeding, and left scary talk to the brain docs who conducted their business deep inside opaque instability.

***

Lift-threatening was clear: we might not make it out alive, or even through the day. The rest was blank and my concerns over blood loss were overpowered by neurologic implications.

I watched the brain doc give me the bad news; he overrode discomfort and contorted his very soul just to get through the conversation. I watched me listen, breathing deep the mist of fear.

He had spoken many times before to families at the same summit of beloved, earnest yearning, and i was not the first father to hope that our family spark would burst forth again from the dust. Whatever stability i had cobbled together was staved in. I literally had to sit.

The worst was not over; it was just beginning. I wanted to flee the scary basement but only wet cardboard stairs offered the lie of escape.

***

The world is full of words and some hurt like spreading sores: *near-death* i knew, but *brain-dead* staggered me. It carried with it the weight of decades of nursing my aging son like an infant—changing his catheter every night before sleep, rolling him to prevent skin ulcers and endless sponge-baths to remove the reek of urine and decay. Somehow, while my weary body grew older i would move his inert flesh, yet again, from bed to wheelchair and back again.

I had cared for a paraplegic man when i was younger and remembered above all else how heavy it was the body that could not move itself.

> the other cold shower this morning was when they stopped the fentanyl sedation drip to see if felix was at all responsive. he was not.
>
> he did not react in any way to any of us calling his name loudly ...or to any other mildly painful stimuli. he remains too deep beyond the veil, and we must continue to wait.

I tried to hurt my son; i wanted to. It would tell so much. I pinched his biggest toe with all my fear to make him cry out... absolute zero. We were near death, and death was near and taking form, but it revealed nothing to my constant wide-eyed gaze; it waited, tall in the hallway, six feet from our room. Dark ethers bleached the curtains covering the sliding glass of the ICU door.

No One Knows!

I had my mantra: *no one knows*. Not paramedics, nurses, doctors, orderlies, technicians, family nor friends. Not one person i met could tell me what would happen, even seconds from now. No one could assure me that Felix would survive one minute to the next.

In the emotional battlefield that was my brain this universal ignorance was of small but significant comfort. I built a totem to our uncertainty and when i imagined him wheelchair-bound for life, this sacrament allowed me to outrun despair.

The *worst*, i wanted to yell at death, may never come to pass and even *you* don't know what will happen when!

***

I willed Felix to live, but so what!? *Everything* was bigger than i was and i struggled to accept; i waged a simple fight against annihilation and turned away from featureless surrender.

My will's desire for my son's survival smashed up against the urge to let Life unfurl itself as it will. I felt far from powerful. My words struggled to build the reality i tried to create.

> i have been relentless (in a gentle way) about gathering information. i talk to everyone!! and from this range of sources (doctors, nurses, respiratory techs, lab people...) i piece together a mosaic of the truth.

For 3 or 4 hours after talking with the neurosurgeon i absorbed the new words into the patter of my *right now*, and adjusted contemporary reality to barely manage not suffocating under the fear that offered itself to me so completely.

> the notion of being present, in this moment, has been the practice that has sustained us. the fears are endless and the hopes are false reassurance.

I played with words: *life-threatening* i could barely write; be strong my father-self told me. But i couldn't bring myself to put down on paper for all time the words that threatened most: *brain-dead*.

CHILDREN LIVE

"I tell you the truth, unless you change and become like little children, you will never enter the kingdom of heaven.

Therefore, whoever humbles himself like this child is the greatest in the kingdom of heaven. And whoever welcomes a little child like this in my name welcomes me."

JESUS, MATTHEW 18:3-5, NIV

JUNE 4 | DAY 3

On Monday, after being safely ensconced at Jane & John's since the fall, the girls came to ICU to greet their brother, and try on their new life.

There is a picture of Hanna from that time, standing by her brother's bedside when Felix was still comatose and the darkest clouds had not yet gathered. I looked at that picture many times in the months that followed, but it wasn't until years later that i saw how tired she looked. The dark circles under her older-too-soon eyes had escaped my gaze for so long. All i had seen was her smile. I needed that smile.

Hanna was strength, grounding and vitality in the face of grave threat to our family and her beloved brother. I was so grateful to my brave 8 year old girl for holding up so well. I had so little to give, and it would have crushed me if she had collapsed under the strain. She did not, not at all.

Hanna came to Felix's beside that first Monday and was solemn. She touched him gently, held his hand through the interventions and told him he was going to be OK. She was quiet, likely prayed. Hanna was making plans by then, for how she would help. She restrained tears and gave us all of her own fire.

> hanna today met w/ a child life specialist. the lovely woman had hanna pour out details of felix's life, thoughts for his recovery, and she was so sweet in her depth of caring for the wellbeing of felix's sisters.
>
> it was so dear to feel that hanna too was healing from this. she holds felix perhaps closer to her heart than anyone, and this for her has been very traumatic. she saw him fall, and was the only family member there when it happened. hanna and saskia are doing well.

I wanted Hanna to be healing too, so i wrote it, but words were poor substitute for actually helping her directly, which i tried to do whenever we were together; sometimes, though, words were simply masks.

Saskia kept a more quiet vigil. She would stand at Felix's bedside, her four year old eyes pouring out love into his face, willing him to get better. She would then leave, and explore the rest of ICU. Not her body so much, she would use her mind and soul to help her brother heal. Saskia was wise company in the realms of uncertainty; i am ever grateful for her young and elderly companionship.

THEIR WORK HAD BEGUN

Saskia and Hanna held space for who Felix was before the fall, and for who he might be again. They assembled onto a big yellow poster board the boy we hoped lived beneath the heavy tossed blankets of his wordless coma: likes, dislikes, hobbies, favorite foods and colors.

Neither Tina nor i could have answered those questions: what does he like to eat? *Anything!* Please, just let him eat again.

We adults saw too clearly the shaded possibilities and grieved, setting our pain alongside the duty we had accepted as parents to be present and care for our fallen child.

Being present did not require looking back to how our lives used to be; the girls held that space. We were present in different and staggering ways. They drew pictures of late-spring flowers while we stood fast and tried not to succumb.

***

A few days later we tore our eyes from the bedside long enough to behold the girls' graphic contribution to our family's healing. His favorite movies were Harry Potter and Zorba the Greek, and his favorite activities were playing piano and climbing trees.

Their work made Felix bigger in the world of the living, a boy we prayed he'd inhabit once again.

The rest of Monday was calm. His hematocrit stabilized and no further transfusions were called for. The seepage of CSF lessened, his skin tone improved and he appeared tranquil. He looked as if he were resting deep.

They ran an EEG and the results were the complete absence of bad news—no word about stroke, aneurysm or necrosis. They confirmed what we knew, that Felix had suffered a major trauma to his brain and his condition was critical.

in gratitude

fear and anticipation
we lived in flesh.

Joy, too, was experienced
as electricity mesh,
and the spaces between.

Moods shifted
and will
stirred first.

Did cells cause,
or merely look up
to behold
the stars beyond counting?

Was the mind's journey
of any concern to those
hard at work
being stunned,
and determined to survive?

ILL WITH EASE

If I ventured in the slipstream
Between the viaducts of your dream
Where immobile steel rims crack
And the ditch in the back road stops
Could you find me?

Would you kiss-a my eyes
Lay me down
In silence easy
To be born again?

VAN MORRISON, ASTRAL WEEKS

THAT FIRST MONDAY

By now i was used to fear seeking lodgement, an inner smog, ill-fitting but wrong, and neither. Sadness was the new norm, despair took a room and i craved rebirth. Please.

Time and again i tried to see what had befallen us in the best possible light, which helped me endure the long minutes between the chances i got to pay attention. The burdens were large and i wished to lay no more stones upon the scale.

I found that choosing gratitude made less room for fear, and kept terror twice as far away. Committing myself to finding good in each moment was something i *could* control. The more i thought life in ICU was OK, the more it became so, but finding OK was complicated. It had many moving parts.

Any moment that seemed destined for rejuvenation was often as quickly arrested by the urgent desire of life to live its own way. I wrote, with high density and low punctuation:

> latest update is that the 'crit is stable, no sign of infection, feeding tube inserted over night into the jejunum, and they started giving him food (through the tube) for the first time since the fall.

He had a 'bolt' in his skull to monitor intracranial pressure, a breathing tube to push oxygen to his lungs and another tube to draw excess fluids and debris from his chest. A gastric pipe sucked blood and waste from his stomach and a bunch of iv's, probes and monitors pierced veins, arteries and innocence his whole body over.

They had drilled, using power tools, a temporary seven-inch steel rod through his lower thigh and it stuck out on both sides just above the knee. To this they attached a complicated set of pulleys, ropes and scaffolding to keep his leg in traction while they waited for his brain to stabilize so they could operate on his comminuted femur.

We were told by some that we'd be two weeks in ICU, then eight weeks of insurance-funded, in-patient rehab; grimmer contingencies were also discussed.

**

Being present, to use Tara Brach's enlightened wording, required *radical acceptance*. Another phrase from a distant time fit as well: *unconditional surrender*.

Accepting was not a singular event but a continual reaffirmation that i was willing to endure anything, moment by moment, undyingly committed to staying present.

By surrendering unconditionally for my son, space opened to create meaning from this experience. I did not yet know how to change the outcome, but i planted precise words and told myself a story.

> we are blessed that felix is a strong 10 year old boy. he has healed and mended himself at every turn.
>
> there have been many tribulations, but grace has been our companion, and the love and support of so many of you has given us sustenance at the darkest moments. it gives felix the help he needs to overcome and heal.

By describing the reality i wanted i hoped to make it come true, for despair destroyed my power to help Felix get better, while gratitude for all kindness magnified the attentive Love that surrounded us.

Thanking the nurse, for example, for giving us 9 minutes of her overdue break seemed to mysteriously inspire the docs to linger in our room a hundred seconds longer, and share with us the angels of mystery that came before bedtime. It added up.

In every measure, when i remembered to say thank you for the best i found in that moment, i felt better and saw Felix as a boy more healing than injured. When the darkness came and came again, this was my private quest, to find gratefulness, even in the face of death.

My faith in our goodness mattered greatly to me, and so i believed, to our wellbeing.

SPUN

By Monday, Tina and i were exhausted. On Saturday our lives had decelerated full-stop, then rocketed off in jacked direction. We found small stability in ICU, familiarity, and within hours, sleep-deprived, it felt as if we had lived there a very long time.

The doctors and nurses told us it was common for the brain to expand after such an injury for up to 96 hours; till then, we should expect little to no responsiveness from Felix.

The notion of a four-day span of expected swelling was comforting: no matter how comatose he remained, we could simply blame it on the normal course of brain trauma. As long as Felix wasn't getting noticeably worse, we had 48 hours left to catch our breath.

***

Every minute those first two days was consumed with assessing, learning, praying, crying, connecting, sitting, holding space, letting go and breathing. By the third day i had a driving need to *understand*—to lay out and behold for myself the myriad details of our new life.

I had always seen myself as 'independent', capable of managing on my own. Asking for help was a struggle—as i never wanted to burden anyone with my troubles—but in ICU our backs were against the wall and i was driven to reach out. I wrote as a humble plea for unsolicited help.

> the absence of bad news here sustains you. felix is severely injured. no amount of prayer can change that. but it could have been worse.

So much of survival in ICU was taking this sanguine mood to heart: cranial pressure was high, but not high enough to operate. His brain was severely concussed, but there were no massive bleeds, and while his EEG showed diffuse brain trauma there were no signs of stroke or seizure.

I wrote because i wanted to find someone who would tell me that it was going to be all right, for despite my brave words, i was scared i was going to lose my son.

***

Monday late i returned downhill to spend the night with Saskia and Hanna at our house. Helpers had stopped by. I came back to find the kitchen cleaned, the girls scared but grounded, groceries in the fridge and a dusty feeling of uncertainty in the air.

Hanna, Saskia and i felt diminished, and *home* was now split between Grant Street and ICU room 13 up the hill.

Tina stayed at the hospital. I was consumed with being drained and catching up with the girls. Over the next eight weeks, Tina and i would spend a total of 20 minutes together at our house—and that time was dedicated to helping Hanna treat an infected earlobe.

One of us was always *on* at the hospital, and Tina was taking the first shift.

HOPE AND FEAR

Fear less, hope more;
Whine less, breathe more;
Talk less, say more;
Hate less, love more;
And all good things are yours.

JEAN BAPTISTE MOLIÈRE

JUNE 4-6, DAYS 3-5

Felix would survive his physical injuries, we came to believe, but we hadn't yet begun asking the new scary question: *what then?*

Scores of minutes lived second by second and he remained alive, without crisis or deterioration, and the names of days blurred, and the clock only told when the next nurse would come. Each shift we asked, if only in silence, *will Felix die?* Probably not, we were told. That was progress.

TAKING STOCK

His condition was critical; the litany of his injuries and the catalog of his medical interventions was our new baseline.

By Tuesday there was small relief, and against the near constant worry i wrote, with all respect, to Felix's young friends:

> felix suffered the following injuries when he fell out of a tree.
>
> - 1 broken, comminuted, compound fracture of the right femur. (comminuted means smashed together; compound means it busted through the skin)

- 1 compound fracture of the radius (near the wrist joint) - this has been set with two pins inserted to help hold the bone together, splinted and bandaged

- 1 small fracture at the elbow

- 1 small chip fracture of the C7 vertebra in the neck

- 2 fractures across the front and side of the skull.

- 1 massive, diffuse brain concussion

but,

- no spinal cord injury

- no lung or rib injury

- no signs of infection

- no signs of meningitis or pneumonia.

Felix's young friends had been reading the web postings since the first and were discussing his fate over countless dinnertime conversations. They were praying hard for his survival, and i continued my chronicle:

he has:

- 1 feeding tube going through his mouth down his esophagus, through his stomach and duodenum and into his jejunum. this is feeding felix 20 cc's/hour of this milky mixture.

- 1 tube in his stomach to suck gunk out (this brought out a lot of blood and dirt and other stuff right after the injury but is mostly clean now)

- 1 large tube connected to a respirator (the breathing machine) which pushes air into his lungs about 44 times per minute [it was actually lower]. it is also used to periodically suction stuff out of his lungs. this was much used to remove blood, dirt, mucous and dead lung tissue during the first 36 hours.

- 1 tube that runs from his arm through his arterial system to a place just outside his right atrium. this is used to deliver the two sedatives (versed and fentanyl). these keep his whole system functioning at a very slow state, so that his brain can be relieved of many of its duties, like breathing and feeling pain. this allows the brain to rest and return sooner to normal size. this tube, the PICC line, also delivers a constant stream of waters and electrolytes (sodium chloride, potassium chloride, etc) to keep his fluid levels balanced.

- 1 foley catheter inserted through his penis into his bladder to drain urine.

- 1 spinal tap, to drain cerebrospinal fluid from his neural system to allow his skull fractures a chance to heal

in his head, he has a 'bolt'—this one is wild. it's a metal tube (literally a 'bolt') that connects from a monitor to a hole they have drilled into his skull. this bolt directly measures the infamous intracranial pressure (ICP). they hope to remove it as soon as they feel the risk of infection to the brain outweighs the information they get.

that's us. blessings, m

MY NEW OCCUPATION

Tracking my son's condition with such assiduous awareness occupied all my mind, and when i allowed thoughts to wander and became unfocused i was easy prey to fear; fear demanded i give up my full attention.

the most valuable lesson, one that is burned into my soul for the rest of my days, is this: in life you have three choices. you can hope, you can fear, or you can be. that's it. the first two are fantasy. only the last is what is really true.

I saw that fear has no innate power, only the vitality we give it. I could take back that power any time and put it to better use.

Fear demanded body and mind and offered information in return, markers to parts of myself that craved witness and held clues. Fear unacknowledged, or coddled, grew larger.

Checking fear became a core responsibility of mine in ICU. My tenacious noticing was aimed at removing any possible place for it to burrow and hide. I was afraid of living life without my son.

I was afraid of the overwhelming sadness that would accompany his passing. I shined light on that pain, called Love to my side and prayed hard for the courage to endure.

***

Tina and the girls looked to me for strength, stability and understanding, and every moment i overcame fear's temptations i made our family stronger.

I realized that despair is fear rooted so deep into my being that it unbalances my body chemistry and addicts me into believing all is not well. I fought that addiction.

I ran through thoughts quickly: hope is fear's cousin and i saw it entice, then dim like the aroma of a safe and distant home. But that which is hoped for is simply another possibility, nothing more. It doesn't exist.

Hope wanted me to *believe,* and yes, hopelessness threatened to wrap me in anguish, but allowing myself to dwell in what might never be was like sitting at the top of a tall tree when the wind blows through, and you realize the tree isn't there any more. I wrote:

> when you choose hope, you must accept fear. They are intertwined and inseparable. when you once welcome the possibility that all might turn out just fine, you must admit that you don't know, and that your worst fears might come true.
>
> you go crazy like that. better i found to simply be.
>
> in the ICU all i knew was that felix was alive!!!!!!!!! beyond that, i would learn more in the next minute, and the one after that. minute by minute, breath by breath, each breath a precious continuation of this amazing life that we all share.

In the end there is nothing but what we have now this instant. And it's enough. Even in ICU i felt serrated joy at this discovery.

WE'VE GOT YOUR BACK

Our lives would have turned out quite differently had it not been for the abundance of love and goodwill given to us by the people of our community. Of that i am certain.

The initial upswelling moved me repeatedly to tears of humblest gratitude. People we had loved for years and those we had only just touched through the tale of our plight showed up to help.

They supported us in person, by word and in gifts left on our doorstep. I was startled how grateful people were to give.

When i began to tell the story in earnest, the first words i had to share were those of *thanksgiving*:

before i start recounting the fall, please, please feel our appreciation for all your good thoughts and loving energy. you have sustained us with every prayer, every phone call, every email, every box of cookies or can of beans or dish of lasagna, every offer to care for the kids, and every sincere offer to do ANYTHING ANYTIME!!!

i truly hope that none of you have to endure the fear we have danced w/ this past few days, but if you are so touched, may you do it with the love and support that we have received. it has literally sustained us and kept us from despair.

During that first week people brought us groceries, took out the trash, trimmed our hedges, weeded, sheltered the girls, cared for our animals, mopped the kitchen floor, cleaned the bathroom, set up personal altars and sat with us at the hospital.

Others left packages at the ICU front desk, created hand-made healing cards and wrote in the online journal. Some researched possibilities, started circles of prayer and chaperoned the girls to recitals or parties. Many reconnected with old friends on our behalf.

Intangible gifts arrived too: free healing sessions, free summer school for the girls, precious self-made paintings, mosaics, books and poems. Countless gifts from the heart streamed into our lives over those first days of trying not to die.

One afternoon before the kinks had been worked out of the online meal calendar, i came down from the hospital to find three families on the sidewalk, two bringing dinner and one proffering a homemade cherry pie. It was enough to bring me to exhausted tears at the bottom of the steps to our pallid, quiet house.

***

Aside from plunging into this trial on behalf of Felix and our family, i pledged to bear witness for the people in our circle, and for anyone anywhere who might need this light. I wanted to find power in facing down fear with courage, and in refusing despair i saw my resolve inspire others. It mattered whether i wrote "trial" or "catastrophe", and whether i remembered to say thank you.

A more awkward task was receiving peoples' assurance that *it will be OK*. Well-wishers, visitors and hallway-seers held great conviction, and at times almost swayed me to belief.

But their *OK* was non-specific: it meant maybe we would walk again, or merely find half-peace inside the tragic confinement of an unending coma.

No one convinced me they could read the future, so i settled back onto that vista-less perch of confidently *not knowing* what would happen next.

***

The prayers people sent were many and sweet, warming slices of sunshine to illuminate the moments between cloudbursts.

> *Felix, we hold you in our hearts and bathe you in golden light. Within you lies great strength and courage—we know you will heal in good time.*

I tried to accelerate each of these precious prayers right into Felix's scrambled brain.

Like the adults, children were urging their friends to pray for Felix; they set up altars, sent us high-touch cards and asked their moms and dads if Felix would be all right.

The young ones sent gifts infused with innate spirit-resilience that i will long cherish, and marshaled their own positive energy on Felix's behalf, peer to peer, and they kept the faith as much as any.

> *Felix, I am taking my copper 'healing' fairy dust and placing it in my copper pot...then I will put it on the fire and make a 'healing wish' for you! My mom and dad have been praying a lot for you, too! Please get better soon! Your friend, Addison*

To their parents i wrote:

> please know that your prayers are being felt. the extra love you show your children tonight is resonating within us in mysterious and magical ways. the tears you shed just brushing close to our pain we feel as healing love.

THE BRAIN

After 48 hours, critical intervention gave way to maintenance—the arduous work of waiting for change to happen. The scent of rejuvenation lived as far off as ever.

Oddly felt at the time, and only faintly known, twin energies of decay and restoration filled the room. Amid flesh sloughing off new flesh was born; we continued our bedside vigil and poured out parental ministrations.

Such rare blinks of healing that we did behold were subtle and in-conclusive, and did not dent our hunger for resolution. They were the un-steadfast vapors of a just-missed falling star.

**

The questions stirred up by the neurosurgeons which i had been able to deflect on Monday, plowed back into my thoughts Tuesday first light.

What if Felix remains unresponsive forever?! What might we en-dure for the sake of keeping our child alive? Was there some line be-tween living and brain dead that we would have to decide?

A friend of ours, father to a girl Felix's age, visited one afternoon. His wife—since a car crushed her, pregnant, ten years before—had lived in a nursing home, in a coma, many states away. She was unre-sponsive to stimuli.

He came to ICU to tell us his story—just in case—so we knew sur-vival was possible, and sometimes came at great price. He came to tell us because we might understand for a moment a few hours of the long ten years he'd just endured.

Countless such stories flowed our way, misery and miracle braid-ed together, but still none could illuminate our singular path forward.

Our Felix was in a coma, and deeply sedated; there was absolutely no way to ascertain his cognition. Every time we probed there was darkness and the same answer to every supplication: *no one knows*.

**

Tuesday morning began in good spirits after Felix's best night of the first three. The nose- and ear-seeping of blood and CSF from his bro-ken skull had slowed, his vital signs were stable and his overall tone, color and presence suggested a boy recovering from deep injury.

In tiny ways, we felt his regeneration in our own bodies. Even though outward signs of healing were few, i could almost hear his damaged bones knitting themselves back together, almost see his torn blood vessels reconnecting their vital pathways and almost feel his cells reorienting themselves to the new tasks of healing, and not cri-sis.

That sweet revery, however, was coldly unmasked by another visit from the neurosurgeons.

> i see neurosurgeons as a sort of druidic sect, dancing close to the mysteries, forever trying to understand the unknowable, but they won't promise anything. they won't give timelines, they merely offer you a range of options as wide as life itself.
>
> the doctor this morning told us felix was in a 'life threatening' situation. After having survived 60 hours of this craziness, i felt we were eligible for phrases one step down from that—something slightly reassuring.
>
> not so. felix might never regain consciousness he told us. we hope he will be able to walk again. we do not know if he will ever be able to care for himself.

Hours of propping myself up with affirmation and clear words were crumbled to shards and my lungs clenched like an arthritic claw.

I prodded for silver lining yet found only fragments of faded wisps. I cajoled myself that the morning's encouraging signs were real, but the spectrum of grim possibility towered above: thoughts of death, paralysis and catastrophic eternal mind-blown debility were common. I wanted to scream.

I wanted to run and cover my ears and punch. I wanted this one crazy nightmare to end. I wanted not to collapse.

***

Staying present meant facing the speculations that arose from the latest neuro-rounds. I had little to contribute to the dialog: anything *was* possible but so what? The sheer range of *what* was deeply unsettling.

I was not able to prevent myself from imagining what it would mean to have Felix unreachable forever. I rolled over on my tongue long inquisitions about what would happen if the spark between us was extinguished forever.

A brief few moments of melancholy saturated me to the edge of despair, and it took strength and determination to return to what was known, knowable and real right then, not what might never be.

> so it goes. small steps. many numbers, little worlds spinning within every blood test, every doctor visit, every change of state.

Little worlds, yes, inside very big ones.

RESPIRATION PER MINUTE

Breathing is a means of awakening
and maintaining full attention
in order to look carefully, long, and deeply,
see the nature of all things,
and arrive at liberation.

THICH NHAT HANH, BREATHE, YOU ARE ALIVE!

JUNE ?? | DAY ??

In ICU the steady pulse of his ventilator was our constant, if cloying, companion. The machine breathed for Felix while he could not, and meant, at least, that his body was still alive.

I, at his bedside, inhaled willingly and knew that ICU was the perfect place to stay real, and watched dread, like sulfurous bug spray, creep about my legs. I breathed out fear and tried not to breathe it in again.

***

Probes tracked Felix's heart, arterial pressure, oxygen saturation, respiration and the one measure—the one number that became the center of our medical universe: intracranial pressure! ICP or, brain vs. skull.

Intracranial pressure measured how distended his brain was—the more it swelled and pressed against the unyielding skull, the higher the number and the more likely it was his brain would crush itself to death.

***

When one of the values being monitored fell outside a set range a distinct audible alert pealed. The foghorn sound was the ventilator's call, more insistent than the "medication finished" chirp. Each warning was distinct.

The signal alarm for high ICP's was a medium-pitched continual tone, a sound that brought immediacy to Felix's bedside, often drawing 3 or 4 ICU staff swiftly from other tasks. Urgent discussions ensued: to counter his swelling brain they pondered a change in the sodium intervention, and discussed draining more CSF through the tap in his spine. They contemplated excising his skull—that brain-exposing surgery we had avoided our very first hour in the hospital.

At times, the ICU workers simply looked on and weighed torrents of cascading information; they silenced the alarm and waited; they watched and prayed just like the rest of us.

***

Whenever in dark hours the ICP alert shrieked, i flooded with adrenaline without consent. My brain was snatch-and-grabbed from sleep and, eyes smeared, i would wake to nurses and doctors hovering about as Felix might be living his last willing breath.

From bedside, muscles gripped, we waited for the crisis to explode or wane, and grew weary of grappling brain-death while watching the long hours age in silence. Felix's bedside was a place, like a playground is, occupying space and naming itself in memory.

THIGH

We still had Felix's shattered femur to repair, and Tuesday afternoon they tapped his spine to release more cerebrospinal fluid: not enough was organically leaking from his broken sinuses to lower the ICP sufficiently to make the operation safe enough.

With that large-needle spigot in place, the brain doctors agreed that the risks from delaying thigh-repair surgery outweighed the risks to his brain from just such a procedure, and the operation was scheduled for the next day.

***

They started leg surgery at 10pm Wednesday. The late hour was not scary at the time, only in retrospect. I didn't think to wonder if they had been doctoring too long, 5am to midnight, and might be less than fresh?

The surgeons drilled four pins into Felix's femur, through leg flesh just above and below the mid-thigh fracture. To these they attached an external fixater, a titanium bar running from knee to thigh-top on the outside of Felix's leg. This was fixed to the four stout pins with medical grade nuts and washers.

Thirty years ago they would have treated a crushed femur such as his with months of traction and bed-confinement. External forces are needed to keep muscle-bound bone from pulverizing itself into each other.

This new hardware would allow Felix to start walking sooner—if his brain recovered enough to manage the task.

> orthopedic surgeons are a world apart from brain docs. they are the engineers, the aqueduct builders, the masons, the grown-up erector set geniuses. they offer guarantees, timelines, promises that you can hold onto.

> he'll have the pins in his thigh for six weeks. after four weeks he can bear weight. they'll come in and look at the leg every two days. after two weeks they will tweak the tension of the bolts (bolts!) if needed.

Their confidence in predicted outcomes was reassuring but did nothing to ease the fear that all steps toward bearing weight might be for nought. Brain fears ruled all.

***

Despite the doubts about Felix regaining cognition, by Wednesday night i felt comforted by an energy of healing that hovered around his resting young body. I didn't see the fading pallor of the slide toward death; rather, he exuded a vibrance that gave flight to the possibility that we would get better. His color was vital and I could feel his presence striving to recover.

LIFE GOES ON

Having a child gravely injured in ICU did not stop the rest of the world from happening. It allowed for a sorting, of course, and effortlessly i ignored bulky strands of our former life. I was irked to find one afternoon a stern, official-seeming reprimand, an unpaid water shutoff-notice tied to the front door of our house.

What remained after winnowing was the need to care for Felix and his sisters. I thought of them constantly, and prayed eternally for their wellbeing.

Hanna and Saskia careened through this on trajectories of their own. I could not follow their life-streams as earnestly as before, and that saddened me. I had always been so close to the heart of their un-furling and here i was distant, during the gravest threat they had ever faced.

The girls and i would reunite after a million hours apart, and i would flip the entirety of my being to catch up on developments in their daily lives. I was deeply curious. I longed to hear stories about the un-injured adventures of two very precious children.

***

About this time Hanna started her own account of *Felix's Fall*. She wrote: 'Felix and Flo were climbing very high. Felix was about to get down when the branch he was hanging on snapped in two. Felix fell down. He landed with a thump, and there he lay motionless on the ground.'

The child life people at the hospital told us that children go through trauma differently than adults. Rather than living it relent-lessly like Tina and i, Saskia and Hanna would feel first, then ques-tion, grieve, suffer, pray, hold space or whatever and return rather quickly to the world of childhood—where play, and what one makes up are as real as anything. It's not that they didn't care as much as we did, it's that their brains were wired different.

Hanna continued: 'Felix's brain was damaged, but only a little. At Jane's, Fiona's mom, we watched Kiki's Delivery Service.'

I never failed to take time with them to discuss what was going on —whether they brought it up or i inquired about how they were feel-ing. We always talked. Sometimes though, utter fatigue overcame and i had to stop and cry in their presence. I could not restrain the tears.

When the topic of Felix and his grave condition was exhausted we moved onto dinner choices, movie decisions and whether or not to go to Goodwill to look for new Barbies.

I came to believe that the girls had neither the background nor the experience to look ahead at what might (or might not) be. Maybe they did. To me, it seemed that they simply knew Felix was severely injured and might die, and in the grand scheme of things, there wasn't much they could do about it.

***

There was no processing time. Since Tina and i were barely home to-gether for two months straight, we didn't have all those late-night kitchen conversations that had kept us connected and up-to-date for years. Everywhere that summer we were busy on opposite ends of the family absorbing huge feelings and trying to serve our son and daughters better than we ever had before.

Saskia and Hanna ended up hearing some of my saddest feelings, the ones that had to come out and came out only when *they* were there to receive them. For their grace, i am deeply grateful.

***

Back at the hospital, i began to see nuances i hadn't noticed before. Felix was *not* utterly unresponsive. He was farther away from us than ever before but something was alive in his broken skull.

His friend Xander came to visit, stayed an hour, talked at Felix then left. He was present, made his peace and said goodbye. It wasn't obvious that Felix was even aware of Xander until Xander had depart-ed:

> within 1 minute, felix's ICP soared from 4 to 26 and his pulse went from 68 to 144. felix seemed frustrated. he seemed vexed that his body or his mind would not accede to his will. it was classic felix. he is a stubborn boy, and can go from calm to not-happy-at-all!! very very quickly. i felt like i was seeing my son's personality for the first time in days.

> i didn't make much of it at the time, b/c i don't want to project my hopes/fears onto him, and lose what is, but an hour later jan (the 'child life' lady) came in and when i mentioned this she said that it was very common for young people to experience this at this stage of head injuries. in fact, it was not uncommon at this point to dramatically curtail visitors, and that's what we'll do.

> so, no more kid visits for a while, at least until felix can relate his feelings in some way other than swelling his brain in mute frustration. adult visitors are fine, b/c like the charlie brown cartoons on tv, they don't seem to register quite the same as his friends do.

***

The temptation rose to see great recoveries in small gestures of strained connection, but repeated attempts to elicit a follow-up response to Xander's visit were met with stone-cold silence.

Felix withdrew, slept, journeyed, checked-out, whatever. Who knows? Maybe his body was digesting the liquid nutrients streaming in and that was enough. Maybe his *relating* synapses were shut down.

Hope, once again, gave way to mute acceptance, a deep breath and the next step of this journey.

> also today felix breathed on his own!! i don't know if it will make it into his chart, the official journal of his progress through time, but the breathing machine stopped today for some mechanical reason. i came into the room to see the nurse david bagging felix—ventilating him with one of those cantaloupe-sized balloon-like bags- and he said not to worry, so i didn't.
>
> they fixed it shortly and all was back to normal. later, david said that while he was bagging he briefly stopped, and felix breathed on his own!!
>
> how cool and amazing is that??? it's likely that it's not enough to sustain his life without taxing his brain at this point, but i take what i can get in the way of direct experience, and that made today a sweet step still further away from the edge.

Like a crack of sunlight under the door sill, he breathed.

LOOK FOR THE HELPERS

"When I was a boy and I would see scary things in the news" Mister (Fred) Rogers wrote, "my mother would say to me, 'Look for the helpers. You will always find people who are helping.'"

I was surrounded by helpers. I desired to be one. People's desire to aid was far beyond our capacity to absorb.

Neighbors, friends and colleagues were so urgently generous, so creatively giving that i struggled to adequately honor their kindness. I offered suggestions for the swelling energies i could not take in:

> - hug your kids and your loved ones a little closer these days.
>
> - call an old friend just to see how they are doing
>
> - share some talent you have with kids in a hospital or old folks in a home. if you want to do it only once and do it in felix's name, he would be proud

- make food for felix and give it to an elderly neighbor, or make cookies for the loaves and fishes people. your gracious offers to feed us are having the unintended consequence that i'm getting a bit tight around the waist. plus, we'll be in this for the long haul, and will graciously accept your sustenance along the hard recovery ahead.

- seek a way to mend any old grudges you might have

- slow down. there's nowhere else to go. we're already here. this is it. this is all we get and it's truly quite magnificent to pick strawberries or smell a peony and hold your loved one's hand...

- draw a wish on a piece of origami paper and fold it into a crane. we'll collect them all and find them a wonderful home

- take care of your community. look around and see who your people are and look inside and see what you have to offer, and be not afraid to share it. if you sing, sing. if you play guitar, play. don't hide any of your amazing gifts from this world.

- if you have a little totem or token that you would like to offer, anything you feel might make felix feel a connection as he wakes up would be welcome...

- plant a flower or tree with blessings for felix and all other families who hurt today...

People took this to heart. Months later a dear friend told me she had rekindled her love of painting because of what she had read, and later that summer she brought us an incredible, colorful outpouring of lovely flowers on canvas. Another friend set up a small altar in the window-sill just behind Felix's bed.

Another woman said she was getting married to her beloved because they had forgiven each other at my urging. People hugged their loved ones tighter, and a few days later a friend delivered 1000 paper cranes to the hospital—each one strung from one of 50 strings dangling from a three-foot branch scavenged from the very same park.

The cranes had been folded one-by-one by students at a nearby school we had never attended. We never learned who produced that sacred project, but those tiny prayers strove heroically to over-fill the ICU.

Each gift was precious, just as each moment tried to be. Each gift fought against the doom as if engaged in cosmic battle.

***

Let Us Hold Faith

I learned to hold space for the love that people were sharing our way, and the healing they were finding in their own lives. Mostly i held space for the present moment, privy to the humbling certainty that it would all come out real in the end.

A fitting poem by Helen Keller found me in ICU, and with tears and countless blessings i shared with everyone...

> *Let Us Have Faith*
>
> Security is mostly a superstition.
> It does not exist in nature,
> nor do the children of men
> as a whole experience it.
>
> Avoiding danger is no safer
> in the long run than outright exposure.
> The fearful are caught as often as the bold.
>
> Life is either a daring adventure,
> or nothing at all.
>
> To keep our faces toward change and
> behave like free spirits
> in the presence of fate
> is strength undefeatable.

***

I held fast against the tenacious persistence of death and studied the electrical outlets around the room. I looked back at Felix and breathed; we were here, still.

In the quiet between breaths, i could not rule out the very real possibility that as much progress as we might be seeing, i might be sitting with the last hours of our son's life.

at the great divide

death he faced
while drugged...

intentional,
but was it bad?

Who's to say
now?

***

Oxygen was plentiful
but canned.

Cells breathed warily,

kerchiefs upheld to filter the
indolent temptation
of opium sleep.

Striving ebbed
as the blood atmosphere
ran with officious mercenaries
sent to poison initiative,
numb pain
and tempt even
those battling for our
very existence.

Under the lure of
narcoleptic death
cells grew weary
of blunt decrees oozing

from reptilian stems
that had taken over
where modern
pre-frontal networks
had failed.

***

A million campfires
dotted ten thousand
smokey hillsides,
lymphocytes staring out
across hand-dug trenches
at veteran bone cells,
each struggling
to find language
for what had befallen
all of us.

Heavy lidded
conversations drooped,
enchantments beguiled
and dark hours receded
to far caverns
deep
in the heart of the mountain.

***

Nucleic shapes
dimmed foggy battlefields
with shadows
everywhere, pebble-cast
tiny shade
as long as generations.

*Light's own exuberance
struck—and struck again
to outshine the darkness, and
often alone*

*pressed full against
the fear of death,*

*like a classroom seed
pushes hard
against the mighty weight
of gentle,
hand-touched soil.*

***

*Cells discussed among themselves
the facing of death...*

*are we riding close, they mused,
or must we stand down in the end?*

*Alacrity fought ennui as
stillness glared down
all movement
save sere ministration,*

*and wasted within
the confines
of his narcotic substrate,
core neurons tried to
remember
how to wonder again
in awe
at the brilliance
of the brain's ability
to know itself.*

ALONE AGAIN

One night I dreamed I was walking along the beach with the Lord. Many scenes from my life flashed across the sky. In each scene I noticed footprints in the sand. Sometimes there were two sets of footprints, other times there was one only. This bothered me because I noticed that during the low periods of my life, when I was suffering from anguish, sorrow or defeat, I could see only one set of footprints.

So I said to the Lord, "You promised me, Lord, that if I followed you, you would walk with me always. But I have noticed that during the most trying periods of my life, there has only been one set of footprints in the sand. Why, when I needed you most, have you not been there for me?"

The Lord replied, "The years when you have seen only one set of footprints, my child, is when I carried you."

MARY STEVENSON, FOOTPRINTS IN THE SAND, 1936

THURSDAY, DAY 6

There was no magic bell Wednesday night to mark the passing of 96 hours—that clear time after which swelling was supposed to subside and we were supposed to be finishing with ICU. Rather, dread infested my pores and the unsavory foreboding that had wavered at the edges of perception since Saturday now bore full into me.

I looked up from the tasks at hand and felt cold nearby.

***

That Thursday Saskia woke from a dream in which Felix was all better and was carrying her around again, a glow that faded fast as observations arrived in fragmented bursts, colored lines and parts of overheard conversation.

Scary things were distorted large, so nowhere felt safe, not bedside, hallway, walking outside, trying to rest... anywhere i went except sleep was dreadful, and even sleep was a bloody mess some nights.

My only choice was to dismiss all that and believe there was something *bigger* still, something made entirely of Love. That was the ultimate grace, and at times i knew it *was* there. Those remembrances would have to carry me through dark times of doubt and back again. My entire fields of perception were frozen in readiness, roadkill-scared, but determined to jump out of the way in time. I just didn't know how.

WE WHO REMAIN

As the day wore on i noticed more animal alertness in my being. The hairs on my skin tingled without warning and my eyes moved over details like a deer scanning the forest when wolves and humans are near.

My breath was harder to find, and suddenly at the foot of Felix's bed a chill shivered my neck. Walking the hallways brought no relief; i was acutely aware of our own danger.

The call to attention was clear: Felix was not continuing to improve. His ICP's were not dropping to normal range and he was no more responsive than he had been the first day. I feared that his body was shutting down after so many days on the bulbous edge.

***

Thoughts of death were frequent; i was not alone in this. Tina began to crumble and the staff would no more smile in our presence. Remembering the trauma of Saturday i wrote...

> i felt i was witnessing that limitless expanse utterly without sound, smell, texture, color or warmth—not death itself but rather, *felix's* death. and it was not the total of felix's death, but rather the backside that i beheld.

I read a Buddhist author who expressed the thought that our greatest fear is not death, but the void of endless loneliness that threatens beyond. That sinkhole loomed close and pulled like dark gravity. Inquiries peppered my thoughts: what if death were truly the end, and my self's total annihilation?

Staring into the shadow of Felix's death—not the death he would experience but the one i would be forced to endure—the emptiness was not abstract. Would Felix's death extinguish the love that he and i had shared so deeply? My introspection rolled on:

> each of our deaths will be intensely personal, utterly unsharable. it is the ultimate solo journey, and that's what makes beholding felix's death from my vantage point so deeply painful.

> after having held my boy a million times when he was too little to walk, too tired to keep going or simply too sad to be untouched,

> ...after having nurtured him and his sisters—as if tending them was the only thing in my life that will ever matter,

> ...after having shared with him the most potent years of my life

> to be faced with the complete end of that is so unfathomably sad.

> i remain so grateful that i have not had to trek through the emptiness of death; my heart and soul go out to every mother and father and sister and brother who has lost a child. i cannot imagine...

I could imagine; death did not offer cherished white light. I did not feel calm or release only sadness no words could describe, and yet i wrote and tried to fathom the seed of grief that was looming down on me.

No Matter What

At some bleary-eyed 3am wandering through ICU i came across a card which had yet to make it front and center. It lay next to a handbill for discounts on scrubs and thanked the staff for helping save their nine year old daughter from death.

Nearby, just out of reach was a note that must have been hell to write, from the mom of a family who had lost their 12 year old to a fall on a mountain-side. She wrote with the same penmanship she had once used to write birthday invitations... *thank you for your heroic efforts.*

One of our nurses told us that he had attended three services in the preceding months for young patients of his who hadn't survived... playful, vibrant children who had ventured too far and left us too soon.

***

I picked up the notice of a memorial service for a different boy who had died. I knew i might have to write such words for Felix. I knew that if he were to succumb, i would have to pick out the songs to be played at his service, and in what order the songs and words would unfurl. I would decide what quotations to include—which to be read aloud, and by whom, and which ones would be merely written into that final brochure of his life and death.

I would have to decide where to hold the service, whom to invite, who should speak, what time of day to have it; i would figure whether to let Hanna and Saskia say something, and while i addressed the assembly, who would sit with Tina while she crumbled under the unbearable grief of having lost her child.

I told myself that i had to think all this through because we were not done with ICU. I had to think it through because Felix was my son, my only son, and no one could take on that task of eulogy but me. I had to think it through because if it came, i would need something to do, some last act of parenting, so that Grief was not alone with me, my hands empty.

We probably would have started with *Ode To Joy* from Beethoven's Ninth Symphony...

...then i couldn't take it any more: no one knows! I looked up through the lowered lights of ICU toward Felix's room and told myself: *stop! don't invent what might never be.*

***

I made my way to get tea in the kitchenette behind the curved veneer of the nurses station. Shaken, i breathed. Tea in hand, i scrambled back over craggy rocks to Felix's bedside and tried to regain the moment. I found him resting, breathing, comatose, whatever! Alive.

I breathed with him, and alone we made it through another dark hour up the hill in ICU room 13.

GOODWILL

By Thursday, Tina and i knew basically what to do. She massaged his feet and i asked the docs questions. Long spans passed. One of us had been full-time on at the hospital since Saturday. There was no other state than on.

Passages of sleep came with dreams, which were noticeable for how quickly they gave way to the near-despair of first waking, a tiny pause to gasp and pivot before the flood crashed back into my unguarded soul.

> thursday, afternoon. today has been hard; i have been crying a lot. i went to the goodwill store with the girls this morning in search of socks. was especially poignant. i often feel broken energy there, rising with dignity to continue this journey. it was comforting.

> i've taken to reading hardy boy books. in them, teen sleuths have clean adventures that always always end well. no one really gets hurt. i read them many decades ago when i was ten.

> felix's intracranial pressure spiked into the fifties this morning. the fifties!! they worry over 25 and it's been mostly under 7. i can only sit with that and imagine his brain swelling so much it bulges out of the skull and down the spinal column... or something equally horrific. i haven't added that to my body of bones today. it's just a wee bit too much.

I tried to hustle the loving energy that was generated when i was with the girls, and transfer it to Felix. It felt like thievish borrowing that i would surely have to repay. What i didn't realize was that the girls were generating surpluses of their own.

> we were riding in the car to the dentist, me and the girls; we were singing the pippi longstocking song, feeling light, when tina called to report that the icp was so high that they were going to do another CT scan to assess. it was a punch to the kidneys. i aged a month of sleepless nights in one breath.

> the girls notice. saskia gauges felix's health by how funny and lighthearted i am. when i'm at ease, i say funny things. when i'm afraid, i get quiet and can't see the way to mirth of any kind.

> then it's just holding on; i so feel for the girls, b/c they suffer this too, and i cannot make it better simply by holding them and putting on another bandaid.

Saskia knew all was not right, but she stood strong and did not flinch. She could not tease out enough nuance to rebalance her soul. She did not have full vocabulary to describe what she was enduring, nor could she create with her words the meaning she desired. Her world was binary: either Felix would die or he would live almost forever.

Hanna was holding up well. She had the support of friends who loved her dearly. She wrote, drew, talked, asked questions and tried to keep the shadows from taking hold. She looked clearly at the sad places then stepped back to childhood. Eight years old was a strong age, and Hanna was a very strong girl.

My fears for a less able future for Felix were too abstract, yet the girls felt my moods, absorbed many of them and still had no sure way to move through the sudden storms with anything approaching ease. They too were making this up as they went along, and i grieved that i could not shelter them from the pain.

Nor could i shelter myself; there was no respite. It was continual onslaught, a firehouse of sadness full on to my heart, no space but to duck and endure.

***

Thursday night on Grant Street was calm. I told myself that his rising and falling ICP's were a sign that he was coming around, not just random misfirings of decay, and i held my breath and hoped he didn't blow his brain out in the process.

The sense of being utterly alone veered unpredictably into moments of calm and perfection. Acceptance, it became clear was not a switch i could flip and be done with. It was a moment by moment practice of knowing and feeling, of being with, of loving what really is and not struggling against.

***

At the time, neither Tina nor i could bear to read the words being written into the online guestbook. I knew they would bring me tears and those tears had other tasks.

Nonetheless peoples' words reached us and were strong bones propping up my sagging limbs, new cells reupholstering my depleted nerves. Each note was an offer to lighten our crushing load.

Friends, and people we had never met, prayed for us with fierce vigor and called upon Divine Spirits to intercede. Adults and children joined together, hundreds of families stitching their lives with ours:

> *Mark: We are all crying with you. I have been praying and crying since I heard the news. When I share Felix's story, we cry together and pray some more. Yet through all these tears, I feel this incredible surge of strength. It is like all of these loving people's thoughts and prayers are holding us up. There is hope. And I feel Felix's pure spirit, so strong. -z*

Like priceless sustenance, the energy they shared was raw and too rich with love to more than sip from without bursting. I was too beaten to absorb more than hour-by-hour survival in ICU.

But i felt every prayer, deeply, and did everything i could to channel that energy right into Felix's broken, unconscious being... and sat, amazed as fibers of lights connected hundreds of us into webs of healing which magnified and humbled my own.

When on a Mountain, Climb

The adrenaline that carried me the first days gave way to a feeling of suffocation beneath unbearable weight. This was not a dream from which i would awaken. We were in it. There was, and is no where, no time, no way to escape. Thursday night i wrote:

> today was hard. i cried a lot. felix's icp spiked two or three times, and was altogether much higher than the last few days. perhaps he's coming around a tad and he notices and reacts to the stimulation more and gets irritated; perhaps he's frustrated that he can't do more. perhaps venus aligned w/ pluto and perhaps we'll never know.
>
> this is where we are. he is still gravely ill. they decided to insert a new arterial line so they could continually monitor his blood pressure; they had discontinued this two days ago. it seems like a small step backwards.
>
> but at this point, measuring every inch gained or lost is insanity. he looks better; he seems healthier. it feels like he is reacting like one could hope—responding to events, getting frustrated, being impatient. or maybe i'm just remembering. i don't know. it is not knowable by any of the 2000 people up on the hill.
>
> i breathe in; i breathe out. so does felix. we live still. we have not crossed over.

> all for now, i'm tired. keep praying.
>
> love, m

On one hand, i saw observable signs of Felix's vibrance. Rather than slipping deeper into the pallor of death, he maintained a healthy color; his flesh wounds were mending. He looked from the outside as if he were healing.

The monitors however, told of pressure building within Felix's skull, a tenacious pulsing that threatened brain-death or total-death with each heartbeat. It seemed that Felix's *Felix-ness* was a tiger sleeping in a cage and the cage was rusting shut forever.

TO THAT LEAF I HOLD FAST

I was back on duty at the hospital Friday evening, planning on one night but ending up there all weekend. I came to know such a feeling of aloneness as never before; yet at the same time there was a visceral understanding that we are all linked, threads of the same garment. I felt connection, not only to those who were reading my late-night words, but to everyone.

> it's between 3 and 4 a.m friday, day seven
>
> i can't sleep. midnight rollercoaster rides do not ease one's worried mind. i think. i watch numbers like a ledge-sitting stockbroker during a crash, wondering if we'll have to jump.
>
> think me not morbid to be thinking of death. it is simply near. it is not my death i fear; that will be its own adventure, and i hope to greet it with eyes wide open and bags packed. it is felix's death i fear, and while we are farther from it (so my simple brain believes) than days ago, what do i really know? it is near.
>
> i was called to pick up the bible yesterday. i read a part and it exploded within me. it was not for me a new passage. it was very very old.
>
> imagine you are walking in a severe valley. the sides are sharp and steep, the path is narrow. the light is everywhere dim, gray and diffuse, almost like a washed out fullmoon glow, but there is no moon, not even the reflection of the sun to remind one that somewhere there is life.
>
> maybe there are shadows; maybe there is scattered sere vegetation. it's not that kind of walk to notice.

the sheer walls tower above a mile, two, ten straight up. there is no end in sight, nowhere to turn back, and up above, on one side, looms a shadow as vast as all the life i have ever known or hoped for, a shadow astronomical in proportion, massive in its gravity, waiting with infinite patience. i am alone.

the shadow ushers forth tendrils akin to iciness—not like the cold that a jacket can ease, nor the fever chills that come from inside. it's an older cold, the cold where life cannot go. i am utterly alone.

even if there were someone with me, there is no comfort. this valley has to be traversed alone.

so i read: "Yea, though I walk through the valley of the shadow of death, I will fear no evil; for You are with me...."

Small joy burst open inside me and tears flowed because i knew fear could not win! Forever, these words... *"I will fear no evil!!!"*

There is nothing more comforting on this trek than to hold against fear. fear comes. it has a life to live, or an ancient promise to fulfill. i stand firm to let evil have no place in my heart, and it's only possible b/c i am not alone.

You are with me, all of you and your precious thoughts and prayers. God is with me, and no matter where the road through this valley leads, no matter how forsaken, there is something more powerful and beautiful and real than death. To that leaf i hold fast.

I am not alone.

Stained Linen

Tina and i had been together nowhere but ICU for a week, and seven days in she started to cave. She was not without a Mother's Love—far from it—but the grief overwhelmed, and her maternal flesh seemed to tear again.

She started to succumb to the fierce icy lashes of eternal loss, and in flight she took the girls and bolted like a refugee for Melody and Brian's for the weekend.

She could not go to our house and smell home and touch the neglected artifacts of our once intact life. In the ICU Felix and i were alone together again, me careening toward the darkest and brightest hours of my life, and as for him, maybe he was just resting.

***

After 96 hours, a gray darkening stasis set in. Stability was no longer the absence of bad news. Now, no news was bad. No news meant we weren't moving off this place of coma. No news meant he still didn't flinch, didn't call out or acknowledge our tears, smiles and mute frustration.

Nurses and doctors aged, grew grimmer and steeled themselves for yet another death, while i craned to behold the bearer of good news and found only empty space.

I suffered the absence of activity and the thrill of constant change that had been my children's childhood. Saskia, Hanna and Felix were three streetcars zooming around the byways of my being, and i was allowed to hop on and off their different, wonderful lives whenever i could. That was the whole point!

Now one train was broken, unmoving, and the rest were stunned and knew we might never start again. We waited, and beheld.

***

There was a plan. The agenda was to keep doing what we were doing, and either Felix would get better or he wouldn't, and we'd leave ICU one way or the other. Maybe rehab, maybe a long-term care facility across town. Or maybe he'd die.

pause.

Cells deciphered
strategic directives
from afar, that distilled
told us one thing:
we must deal.

We wanted nothing less
than total restoration
to how it used to be.

***

Cells obeyed unseen forces,
and death everywhere smelled
like the rancid clean of
an old motel.

To enforce quiescence,
silent
gunmetal
needles
conducted
copious spikes
of
an
-es
–thee
—-zhuh...
direct from picc line to heart,
and heart to brain.

The need to decide was rare.

Whatever speed
had imbued cells days before
was replaced entirely by
a surrender
to knowing that
what will be
already is.

***

Repair continued
on auto-pilot
as vitality yearned and
anniversaries passed without knowing,

and in its wake
urgency gave way
to immediacy
as time slipped
into a guise
no one then living
could reveal.

***

Beneath the chemical haze,
monastic clades of
remembrance cells
girded the eternal flame
like 7th century brethren
hoarding light
on the bracing cliffs of Eire.

So few knew.

The rest...
we suffered blind.

BLOODY TIP

Never give a sword to a man who can't dance.

CONFUCIUS

FRIDAY

There was a standing spot outside Felix's room that held a particular, peculiar energy. It was a crossroads of corridors where one day a friend who was visiting briefly fainted. To her embarrassed chagrin the urgent response team responded, helped and documented what had transpired.

It was on that spot where Tina nearly crumbled in the first hours of our ordeal, and it was a meeting point for many urgent conversations. It was a focal venue for our entire living world, and it dimmed and grew denser with each passing hour.

Mid-day, the intensive care team held a meeting away from our ears and asked each other if it was time to suggest that we consider turning off the life support machines and letting nature have its way.

***

ICU staff did not know any more than we did what was going on inside Felix's mind; perhaps too, they discussed his soul.

Aside from any big picture understanding they held, they were each juggling thousands of particulars every day, and trying every second not to make a single fatal mistake.

They had clues of course, and numbers and experience to build on, but *knowing*... was as impossible for them as it was for us.

The staff felt the nearness of death around Felix just as we did; they remembered other young patients who had died too soon. They saw signs that troubled them to the heart of their ICU mission: keep each child alive. They believed the end for us was coming near.

SUPPOSED

We were supposed to have improved by Friday. The swelling was *supposed* to have gone down a full day and a half before*!* and we were supposed to be looking at a step-down unit then rehab, not considering end-of-life decisions.

> Felix has a fever. his icp's spiked a few times today. his leg is mending. they had to start his spinal tap again to drain out some fluid. a small amount of csf had leaked again from his fractured skull—we had hoped after 20 hours of dry nostrils that the fissures had healed, but more to wait for, more to pray for.

> this journey is weary. one step at a time. breathe in, breathe out. it's what felix and i do together these days. i hope to simply be, and bear witness. your allowing me to share this with you lessens the pain. thank you. love, m

There were no secrets in ICU. We were all temporary inhabitants at the edge of death.

Many young people die in pediatric intensive care. When death is near shadows seep into faces and expressions tell plainly of sadness. Eyes endure, smiles vanish and footsteps slow upon approach, humans delaying contact with the simple confronting of death; the toll would be heavy.

ONE STEP FORWARD, TWO-STEP INTO THE WALL

The immensity of my wishing to know what was coming next was equal to the next moment's reluctance to yield any of its secrets. I studied the situation with a fierce determination to divine its truth, and learned that truth is merely a living moment to experience. All we are offered is the choice on how to live through it.

The Glasgow Coma Scale (GCS) allows trained observers to record a consistent neurological assessment of a person's state, and level of consciousness. It uses a numeric range of 3 to 15 (totally unresponsive to fully conscious and cognizant). Severe brain injury is considered any score of 8 or less. Felix was first recorded at six, scoring a 4 for motor responsiveness—his occasional, ungrounded spasming—plus 1 each (the lowest possible) for his total lack of eye reactivity and utter verbal non-responsiveness. His 6 indicated coma with some movement in response to painful stimuli.

Friday all motion ceased, the brakes locked and we careened to a blunt, deadly halt below. Felix was recorded every hour in the chart as three 1's, the lowest possible. He was officially alive, but totally unresponsive; a segue into death seemed imminent.

I insisted to myself—or was driven by desire, i can't tell—that i continue reading the nurses' notes in the wall-box outside the room. When his observable vitality slipped to 4 then 5 then 4 then 3, 3, 3, 3, 3... each hourly pen-stroke was a slash at my heart. From our already diminished place, we were getting worse.

***

There were other clear markers to assess the failing state of our well-being. Two days before they had split his nurse: Felix went from having one full-time caregiver to having one nurse care for both him and another patient. This was done because he (and the other kid) had stabilized and needed less intensive care.

On Friday they re-assigned him to a single, dedicated nurse.

On Thursday they removed his arterial line because they felt it was no longer needed. I relaxed the tiniest bit and tried to read in nothing, but it was impossible not to feel a lessening of dread. Late Friday, in defeat, they restored the line in preparation for impending battle: more fluids would be needed.

Medicines, stimulants, antibiotics and sedatives were provisioned to be thrown against death in harrowing waves of attack and retreat. They would be deployed through flexible #6 tubing straight to Felix's heart, and from there pumped to wherever they were needed most.

***

In addition to death from brain shutdown, we worried about wildfire blood infection, the kind that starts fast then hits faster. Death can win a thousand ways in 20 minutes, outracing medical genius against which it has gained strategic resistance.

Conversations with nurses ossified and the time-passing vignettes we had shared only hours before gave way to statements of fact. Staff withdrew and shielded themselves from getting too close to a family that soon might suffer the gravest loss of all. They guarded distance yet again to survive their own pain, suffered through till the end of shift and rightly consoled themselves into believing they brought us comfort.

> felix is back to having a dedicated nurse. this seems like a step backwards, but in a marathon, you stumble sometimes.

Within the sadness i tried to see glimmers of light, but they were few.

> his fever is down, and there was a decrease in the white blood cells in his csf, which means less indication of pending or possible infection of his meninges, but his sodium is lower than they wish b/c it's leaking out...

> lots of cultures pending—csf, blood, maybe urine and sputum. no spikes in icp today so far, just steady state since 1 am.

> saskia is having a hard time. she asked why things can't just be normal again. she always asks about felix on the phone, and still worries that he will die. she feels sadness and suffering and misses her big brother and family intact again.

> felix is heavily sedated. everyone wishes that he would come around right now, but the way is long, the outcome unknown, so the only thing to do is appreciate the journey. that's all we ever have, it seems. blessings, m

TALKING TO MYSELF

I tinkered with thoughts and studied reality. I put jumble into words, documenting myself between long bursts of non-moving.

I wondered how different it was for Felix, laying there inert. Where did he travel while i was working so hard to stay sane?

I sat, and watched him unresponsive or walked, and would craft the next journal entry in my head. I would order the events in my mind to see if there was a clue, a pattern, a learning, a way out.

I never 'gave up hope' because i don't remember actually having much hope. That's not to say that i was hopeless—far from it. I just couldn't bear to stand upon thin clouds of what might be. I needed solid grounding *now* and hope did not provide it.

Many people asked about Felix, and as much to find clarity as to respond i held conversations with myself:

Friday night, ICU, he's still unconscious. He is under heavy sedation, and is healing from his physical injuries. His ICP has been consistent for the last 18 hours, and his Cerebral Perfusion Pressure has been high enough to ensure sufficient oxygenation to the brain.

Will he be OK?

No one knows.

What are the possible outcomes?

- He could remain unconscious for the rest of his life.

- He could come out of being unconscious but be unable to speak or care for himself.

- He could come out of being unconscious and have problems speaking and/or caring for himself, but he could function at some diminished level.

- He could come out of being unconscious and regain most to all of his faculties, and live out the rest of his life a hell of a lot wiser than he was last week.

Medical people called this mess a *diffuse axonal injury*; even the name is scary, befitting one of the most devastating types of traumatic brain injury. When i felt brave enough i scoured the web and read: over 90% of patients with this injury never regain consciousness.

What are the chances of each outcome?

The literature shows varying percentages, based on age at injury, length of time before oxygen was given, support of family and friends and the like. One study put 5-10 as the age group most likely to fully recover. Other studies offer less sanguine prospects.

I remember writing that *most likely to recover* sentence. It was phony. In real life i wanted to scream out that Felix had a nine in ten chance of never coming back! I tried to correct course:

You have no idea what will happen with Felix, do you?

Nope, none at all. and that's very very hard to live with.

I continued making up the exact questions i needed to answer.

You seem to have a thing with fear, don't you?

I hate fear, actually. And I'm not talking about the kind that gets you running from avalanches or rampaging hippos, but the nasty kind that invades your soul and offers nothing but despair. i haven't yet seen a redeeming side to that part of this universe. I will fear no evil. I love that. A two'fer. No fear. No evil. :-)

What's your current strategy for dealing with fear?

Well, there's present-time living, which i mentioned earlier. I discovered another one today.

Tina called from the hospital all distraught b/c she had seen one of the docs shake his head and look sad in response to a question about felix she didn't hear. it's that easy to fall into.

we talked about how no one, and i mean no one(!) knows what will happen with felix. he's a lovely, robust, spirited child who is shrouded in so much love i cannot even fathom. all that helps, but doesn't guarantee anything. he is healing his wounds, and he's not totally vegetative. so the strategy is this, and it pissed off fear when i discovered it.

when fear comes and whips your head, heart and soul around with utter disdain, when you are twisted into tears and chest-crushing anxiety, you actually get a free pass into hope.

for every breath you are forced to endure fear, you get to have that much hope. it's a law of nature or spirit or something. fear doesn't want you to know it but once fear's shadow cuts through you, you are permitted to have hope, in at least equal measure.

i still find it more sanity-inducing to stay away from both hope and fear, but this has helped.

By equating fear with hope i saw both as ephemeral; it made what remained less scary.

***

I stalled; death was big enough so i fell back on honesty. Fear was not malign; it was messenger and behaved like it had to. Me? I took blows. I continued to ramble to keep myself company. Words gave me space. I imagined how the girls were surviving and strove to fortify Tina while exaggerating her ease in my thoughts. In ICU space was rare—machines and fear pressed in on all sides.

How are the girls?

Hanna seems to be doing better than i would have hoped. she has a good personal support network, and a great ability to express her feelings and at the same time be strong in the face of adversity.

Saskia is bereft and without anchor. she suffers from life out of balance, family in trauma, and i cannot make that better. it's humbling, difficult, stressful, sad.

How is tina?

she is doing better. she has found a path and if she keeps to it—to the present moment—she too survives. despair comes, but then we hope together. we are alive in this. it is hard.

What's so great about the 'present moment' during a trauma?

the possibilities that branch out from this trauma are so vast, that it is burdensome to try to hold them all. the fears, the hopes, the paths we could be asked to walk.... it's massive, tangled, enticing, wicked and raw all at the same time.

who has the strength, wisdom or fortitude to withstand all that?? not i.

i find the weight of all the possibilities unbearable so i simply stay present. i can deal with this breath... and this one. when the time comes, i'll endure whatever breath comes along. that's life, that's all i have.

I thought back to Thursday morning, 36 hours before... Tina massaging Felix's feet, singing to him, while i told him stories and plied him with updates from life outside the ICU. By Friday night all that was gone, and there i sat not quite alone.

EMBERS

*The wave is part of the ocean
just like Grace is part of everyone.*

*You can't take the Grace
and put it in a place
that's different from all of creation.*

*Let me say it like this:
Love and the living are one.*

WAH!, MA CHANT (KALI)

FRIDAY-SATURDAY

As our seventh day came to a close, Tina's growing awareness of the sanctuary of the present moment was not solace or power enough to cradle her from mother's grief. She hurt too much.

She withdrew into an anguished old-world shell as the pain gnarled inside her. It hurt me to behold her; i could only imagine how awful it was for her to be living through this as Felix's mom.

I felt her misery as pain at least one level deeper than my own, acutely aware that it was *her* body that had nurtured Felix from the very first. I sent her what sanctuary i could, but it wasn't much. Days later she wrote online for the first time—i'm sure with tears in her eyes:

> Dear friends, This morning i looked at the website for the first time since Felix's fall. It is so good to hear all your voices! Please keep sending healing energy and prayers Felix's way, we all (and I) need them so badly! While Mark has found such a strong voice amidst all this pain, I am often struggling with keeping the ground under my feet and breath in my body. I so

> miss my little boy. Please help me breathe, help me have faith and strength to get through this. Tina

The strong voice she saw in me was a projection i vowed to continue. I tried to spawn thoughts that were not horrific. That was practically the whole point of my existence... to choose. I couldn't stave off death but i could choose how to behold, and to seek beauty.

Such nuance meant nothing to Tina's mother-despair. I could feel her unveiled sorrow in my own body. Felix's death would be a slow, endless blow from which she would never recover. Of that i was certain.

In small ways i was glad she had fled the grim frontline of ICU; i needed to be alone, on duty, and the fewer people i had to focus on the better.

***

I watched myself prepare for the death of our son— a few last hours to sort out ten years of everything. I thought i heard a gigantic weight shifting on cosmic scales; a tipping point was near and the outcome would not be in our favor. I saw us as a sad part of life's vast unfurling, and i was powerless to avoid its path.

Nonetheless, i reminded myself every chance i remembered that we had survived one week. We were still alive, still in the midst of our trial and hadn't been asked to cross over. That was core true and i returned to the work of being now.

THE BLADE

Friday night was interminable. Sleep clawed at my eyes, pulling me down for brief bouts of restlessness. The chair knew every contour of my body. The monitors pierced my dreams like train whistles and frequently i was clutching at Felix's bed rails touching, looking on, making sure he was still alive.

The ICU staff tried to balance sedation and its subterranean ability to keep the body still, with the need to wean the brain and assess any remaining cognition.

Sedation was cruel comfort, allowing us to adjust, to make peace, but there was a cliff's edge realization that withdrawing from the drugs would reveal the truth.

Around 2am Saturday Felix pooped. It had been a week since his bowels had last moved and it was so prodigious that his nurse called other nurses over to behold the epic size of his stool.

In the wake of that small intestinal normality, my mind rummaged for phrasing that would crystallize my feelings into tangible blessings, something i could offer and reflect upon, a burden i could share. I sought a proper naming for the sadness.

***

Many eyes served us; many observed. A friend wrote poignantly Saturday morning that we were on the tip of the sword...

> this feels quite true. sharp, no room to stretch out and relax, bloody mess for any misstep, the first to take whatever contact lies ahead.

> but if we are on point, you all who support us and pray for us are the body of that sword, the strong fine steel that gives us heft under our feet, gives us grounding and weight and leaves us not a dot floating in space, but a part of something clean and beautiful.

We had mass: mere words perhaps, but they gave me power. To see myself on point but not alone brought a moment's ease, and a sense of raw strength—a sip so that i could stand strong once more.

The words and silent prayers excised pain from my near despair, and served as counterweight to the plumbless fathoms. They helped me re-balance, so that i could humbly breathe again.

***

Others felt it too, this sense that we were involved in something bigger than any of us alone, that we were drawing from a source older than death. We were creating something born of Love.

> *mark ~ tina ~ felix ~ hanna ~ saskia*

> *you are all being cradled by a community of people so full of strength love and light. we will carry you as you navigate this unfamiliar terrain. we will be behind you shining our light as you find your way through this darkness. collectively, we are sending forth energy and intent from an endless well. take from it. it is there for you.—a*

I marveled at the abundance from which i was allowed to draw. There could be no greater gift than these magical blessings.

I KNOW FELIX

I knew Felix as my son—the only boy i'd ever held within minutes of his birth. I knew him as brother to his wonderful sisters, a central, buoyant, rambunctious ten year old. I loved him so.

I wondered, as i gazed upon him from the bedside rail, if we would ever explore again, if we would ever re-visit that one postal building downtown with the cool glass elevator, the one we used to ride up and down on random Saturdays. I missed him so.

***

Lots of us missed him hard. I had not known so clearly before the impact he had made upon people in our community. In similar situations i know families would support each other, and a lot of people were supporting us as a family.

But even though he was just ten years old, Felix had made distinct impressions upon a number of adults and children alike. People spoke so dearly about the boy they missed.

> *Felix has sung in my children's choir for a couple years, and is such a joy to me with his energy, joy, playfulness and musical talent.*
>
> ---
>
> *You are such a special, vibrant boy. I know if anyone can pull through such a trauma, it is you!!*
>
> ---
>
> *He is a true gift.*
>
> ---
>
> *Everytime I've seen you, you run up to greet me with a warm hug, and share with enthusiasm a new invention or art project, story, or joke. This seems to be exactly how you greet the world, which is truly a beautiful blessing.*

I was struck by people's sense of *Felix*, recollections of his kindness toward younger children, his infectious smile and enthusiasm. They missed Felix. We all did.

THE GIRL IN THE RED CHERRY DRESS

Life ripped me raw and shredded me to the mere magnificence of being alive. Torn through, i perceived pure life with breath-taking ease... lightening flashes of profound clarity then gone, shadow-memories of Perfection.

Realization transpired too fast to articulate, like spying a hummingbird darting rainbows against the high sun of noon. I knew in starbursts that everything was, and is, completely All Right.

***

Seconds later storms raged back, drenching me, crowding away happy thoughts and shortening all horizons back to the scary place called *now*.

Darkness struggled with core understanding to keep faith and hold tight. Do not fear what is to come.

None of this meant Felix would survive, or recover, or think or walk again. I knew those desires well. It did mean however, that in all sadness all was not sad. I felt keen joy alongside pain. Pretense was gone, artifice abandoned; there were no longer filters to wear. I looked a mess, my eyes were bleary and my face was red from crying, yet i saw with such untainted ease...

> there was a girl in the elevator a day or two ago when saskia and hanna and i were riding up to see felix. she lived in a body shrunken like that of an old woman; her head would have seemed small on a newborn, but she must have been somewhere between 7 and 12. she was wearing a bright and beautiful spring dress and i said to her in the crowded elevator "that's a lovely dress you are wearing."

> she brightened at once to have been noticed, to have someone see her as touched with beauty...

Or maybe she smiled simply to be kind.

> she smiled at me and said in a voice squeezed out of a voicebox too small "yes, it's cherries."

> "cherries," i said, "how wonderful in springtime to wear a dress with bright red cherries on it."

> "yes" she said, "i love cherries..."

> our floor arrived and we stepped out. i wished her a wonderful day and she beamed back the same wish for me; the elevator door closed on our togetherness and we moved on with our lives.

My blood skipped as i wondered who lived in such a body? I wondered if she still believed in some corner of her heart that she'd meet her prince, one day find her princess and be asked to dance, one day be lifted into her lover's precious arms? I wondered if she'd ever be told she is *the one* to make someone's life complete.

> who is it that speaks in words hard to hear for they sound like the misshapen song of an old man? who is it that lives in a body that scares the other children for being so different, who lives in a body that many recoil from for fear of contagion?

> i know who lives in such a body. it's a little girl in a red cherry dress, breathing in and breathing out the days of her life, just like the rest of us.

I think of her often, her bright smile, her quick connection, her sincere wishes for me to have a wonderful day.

Wherever you are i hope you too have a wonderful day! I hope you don't find me naïve. I feel forever blessed to have met you, to have seen with you for a moment with these tired eyes, the true magnificence of what is.

grieve

now,

surrender was mandatory...

every cell
thundered
into doing
her work... Grief,
for
she had will
to do;

all aligned
to her bidding and
bent beneath
the massive pulses
of her breeze,

trees blown flat
in a volcano's
primal blast.

Tissues succumbed
and produced
in spasms
the very grief
we mortals feel.

She struck everywhere.

***

Furrowed muscles
fired at her contraction
and emptied lungs
of all breath.

Grief was serious.

Diaphragm gasped
and inhaled
what felt like last air,

as barricades opened
and let flow
fears ripe
for shedding.

***

Molecules made
other plans, sought
new hosts
and hoped
to be called again
to comprise
the body of
a single
lively soul.

***

Then, in the reverb
of that first wave,
cells rushed back
in unison as
sobs crashed out

and mass flung itself
toward solid ground.

Phosphates gone,
fatigued muscles stopped

—without power
function ceased and
gravity demanded
i crumple to
to Mother's embrace.

Grief was serious.

***

Like the million year echo
of the first word,

Grief flooded through
and washed me clean...

and from repose,

amid death,

i looked up
and wondered
not why,
but how

and when?

LIFE HAPPENS

really!?

THAT SATURDAY

Stimuli rained down from all sides—little things like the catch in a nurse's voice or the side-long, low-contact glances of the attending physician. It all amped me, and shook me like a mad housewife beating a filthy rug.

The last thing i wanted was to drive us at high rates of speed over the cliff. Death was the blackness beyond. I had to do, not-do, and i knew not which or how much of either.

***

I felt Tina's sadness and knew mine was greater than any before. Each hour comprised 60 minutes and each minute melted along for a million seconds unless it evaporated first in a dusty puff before i could duck. Each instant made way for the on-coming locomotive of the next.

I wondered if the girls were OK? Was there anything i could do to help with the pain we shared, as we had once shared cookie-baking and storytelling.

My family's wellbeing was uppermost, as were medical updates, doctor consultations, gifts and stories to accept and acknowledge, replies to write and read, arrangements to juggle, and one injured boy to love in the bed to my side.

For my own sake, i continued sharing with anyone, anywhere, and people sent our story around the world. Countless souls generated healing for us to hold and sustain on Felix's behalf.

> some of you tell us felix will be all right. you say it with conviction, and at times, with a knowing that extends deeper or farther than we can see.
>
> we cannot go there, but please do so for us. please plant that seed in your soul and nourish it with every bit of your being that you can spare.

When people told me it would be OK, i wanted to believe that they were seeing into a future to which i was blind. At the same, i forbade myself from going to that place where all might turn out OK. I needed to know both, and the happy thoughts were easy. It was the rest that offered cold refuge against the storm.

Hours before i had experienced eternal perfection, and now i contemplated death beyond time. I wanted to participate with Felix again in the Miracle. I wanted more than the avoidance of death. I wanted life! With my entire self i wanted Felix to heal completely in every way.

By Saturday, death was closer. I bargained from my heels and flailed not to drown. I battled my own disintegration, and called upon Jesus to help my son.

***

Twice before i had called to him, to Jesus, and both times he came directly, and instantly helped. Jesus arrived during losing bouts with enemy spirits during the intense PTSD after the robbery.

I recalled the first time... my thoughts were filled with demons yelling, as if my head were a vast, smoky, underground cavern, and on the walls of my torch-lit mind were perched thousands of fiends, all screaming shrewd hatred down upon me. They targeted my deepest dread and left me shrinking beneath their menace.

I was surrounded, petrified and saturated with fear. Without forethought i desperately and deliberately called Jesus to my side. *Please help!* As promised he came quickly! Every demon fled like light leaves when the switch is killed, and cowered beneath a *loving grace* far greater than they could understand.

In the penumbra of that cavernous hall, Jesus protected me, fear lost and in post-chaos exhaustion i collapsed in tears. A mountain moved off my soul for i was safe, and not without power. I remember feeling as if i were with an an older brother who loved me beyond sorrow. I called to him once again decades later from the bedside:

> i asked jesus simply that he help felix overcome so he can go on being his lovely, sweet self. i told him that the world will be a better, more loving place with felix in it, and i said that when he's better, say a year from now when all this is a wise memory, me and him and his sisters will go back up to ohsu and he'll play piano for all the kids who have cancer and are living so close to death.
>
> we'll go up there and hanna will make gift bags for them with stickers and special beads, and felix will tell them stories and show them his scars and smile at them... i promised jesus all those things. i hope he will help.

In response, nothing that i could tell was different—we were not done.

***

Saturday morning Tina and the girls left their isolation at Melody's to come to ICU. I was too derailed to offer support of any kind. The pain was too great for Tina and they left after 45 minutes.

Hanna's best friend lived at the house where they were bunkered, so she had companionship. Saskia was left out, and not having her mother to lean on, she was very sad. I tried to offer her comfort before she left the hospital but i was bereft.

> saskia and i have spent the last few years sharing a rich fantasy life, filled with princesses, doctors and accordion players, glorious costume balls and menageries filled with animals who have needed our special care.
>
> the past week this wellspring within me has dried up. i don't have the space to build a world where a happy ending is assured, where we can be free to imagine ourselves however we need to be.
>
> she has been watching me this past week.
>
> when i am far from fear and able to smile, she relaxes, steps back and lets childhood return. when i cry and cannot keep her from it, she hugs me as tight as she can to hold me up, and then slowly returns to knowing that the sad story is still going on and we're in it and i can't make it all better by simply telling her that

"once upon a time there was a girl named saskia, a girl named hanna, a boy named felix, a popi named popi, and one day..."

and one day life happened, and this is where we are.

DESPITE THE SADNESS

My spirit came to you, and you accepted me.

THE AUTHOR, TO HIMSELF

SATURDAY-SUNDAY

As antidote to the frequent bursts of gloom, i honored peoples' blessings by documenting what we were going through, and by widening
the circle to make room for others to learn from journeys of their
own.

THE RIPPLE EFFECT

People were glued to the midnight Caring Bridge updates; replies to
my posts came back within minutes.

People found resonance in their own lives. They were weeping
with us, thanking us and feeling this living tragedy deeply in their
own bodies. Folks touched their own traumas in empowered ways,
looked at old wounds unresolved, and began to move through shadows in a healing way.

I was determined that even if our tragedy grew larger, something
good would come. A traveling friend reflected:

> *I am here in oklahoma visiting a friend whose husband died
> suddenly. It is clear in these times of intense pain, what is im-
> portant, and how powerful love is.*
>
> *We all are so connected that if we stop we can feel it. It is at
> these times perhaps we know it most. –g*

Slowing down to behold that majesty was light across our shadow.

***

We began to avail ourselves of the many offers for direct healing and therapeutic help that had come our way, from chiropractors, massage therapists, Reiki practitioners, acupuncturists, naturopathic physicians and a Native American trained Shaman.

That Saturday we invited a dear friend, our family chiropractor, to come to the hospital to see if he could aid in Felix's healing. Felix had been going to him for tune-ups half his life, so Dr. Larry knew his spine, body and spirit well.

All five of us over the years experienced great ease after receiving Larry's healing care, and falling from the tree, Felix had undoubtedly suffered a traumatic compression to his entire body.

His neck, head, vertebrae and sacrum (among his other injuries) were obviously sheered, so we welcomed gentle ways to bring length and balance to Felix's spine. We knew it would aid whatever healing was our due. From notes that Dr. Larry kept that Saturday:

> *My first visit to Felix was June 9, one week after the fall. He was in ICU, coma, immobile, breathing apparatus. Life and death were on a precarious edge at that point. With Tina's permission I lightly palpated Felix' right upper neck. As his CSF pressure was still spiking at that time, I took care not to contact his occiput or any part of his cranium.*

> *His first cervical vertebra (C1), palpated as pronounced lateral to the right. I took a light contact with my little finger, and altered the direction of my finger until I felt the vector was correct. The amount of force was probably as much as you would need to touch your eyeball with your eyelid closed, and feel it.*

> *I held this contact for several seconds, released it, then repeated 3 times.*

> *Briefly, the upper cervical region of the spine is one of the areas in which a small amount of local intervention can effect a large degree of global change, both structurally and through its effect upon the nervous system. I felt that even though it was what might appear to be a minuscule effort, at least it was able to address a crucial region.*

From that small seed, perhaps, restoration began its weary ascent.

The Shadow of Death

Most of what occurred was beyond choice. All i had was now and how i showed up to everything.

At times i could choose how to feel about what i felt. I could choose where to put my attention and could intend to endure with grace and humility. But i couldn't choose to grieve or not.

> saturday night. i am in great despair. i feel the shadow of death nearer. i hesitate to write, but i must bear witness to something, and in so doing, make an offering to the spirits of kindness and love.
>
> felix is not continuing to improve. they removed him from his sedation, and so far, he has not responded to any stimuli. this is worse than it was three or four days ago when he flinched and stretched his leg. there is now more talk of diffuse axonal injury.
>
> the doctors look more worried, and express their thoughts in less sanguine words, longer faces. today's nurse said that he was worried, and when asked said that some kids die from these injuries. the brain just can't deal anymore. some stay unresponsive. some begin to respond but forever require care. some do recover, but... there are a lot of buts now.
>
> i wish i had something to hold onto tonight, but i don't. your love and support has been invaluable, but in this valley, i am alone. please do continue to pray for felix and our family. i was feeling such deep sadness for my son tonight, imagining how it might feel for him to be unable to command his body to act like it did a mere week ago. how much he might long for simple things like hugging his family and eating sandwiches at home.
>
> please do continue to pray, and hope, and make cards. they all say they just don't know what will happen. we know tonight what might happen. we feel the shadow of death near. it is cold. i do not like it. it is a place without life, but it shows us nothing more about what might be. felix is a mighty soul and spirit. perhaps tomorrow will push back the shadows again. tonight we breathe in and breathe out, and are sad.
>
> blessings to you all! m

Saturday night wouldn't end. I took a midnight walk to escape, and 5 minutes in i collapsed, and all of me wept and grieved beyond control. My lungs heaved new air in and old air out.

I stood, righted myself. I walked to the next lamp-post and broke down again. I stopped and leaned into the pole to keep erect. Tears streamed without measure.

Eventually i made it back to the hospital, where the cold front entry of the dark tower was locked. I had arrived at Oz and the weird green door was thirty feet off the ground.

I couldn't see Felix's window for all the cement, but i did find a button to push and after a long pause was asked to state my business: fate ordains my presence, i whispered. I was allowed entry again.

I returned to Intensive Care, fully at home, dreading death, dreading the after-death where we all live and grieve and perpetually miss our boy.

***

I breathed with Felix and his machine, and watched oxygen bleat into his seemingly inert body. I gasped at small sips drifting by to exist a few seconds more, and bathed Felix in as much coherence-enabling love as i was able.

I sought the crucial tendrils of his conscious soul to grasp onto, but like a lost child in the wilderness, i wandered numb farther into the forest. My calamity was too vast: to which of his trillion assaulted cells should i direct my call?

Felix and i could not talk or hug or smile; we could not run or eat or plan. We could only be still, and mourn. We were both called to patience; he lay there and I grew exhausted.

Being patient i learned, implies waiting—for something, and i saw only scary things ahead. Even putting Felix back on sedation as they did overnight Saturday because he was flinching again in pain seemed irrelevant.

> sunday morning brings sunrise, at least a bit of light.
>
> it feels as if we have fallen much lower. a new feeling is infiltrating me that things will never be the same in our world. felix may never play piano again. He may never be able to feed himself or talk or walk.
>
> a few days ago these seemed abstract possibilities. there was so much else going on and we hadn't gotten to any tipping points. he seemed to be progressing. now it seems we have entered a time of great sadness.

i still admit that anything can happen—we have heard many stories of people coming out of terrible situations like this. but we also hear, and watching felix can see, other paths, where recovery is measured in tiny steps along years of healing and retreat.

we do not know what the future will bring. i wish this were fear that i was feeling, b/c then i could flip it off. but it seems more like the turning of a season, simply a state of being that happens and we are all in it.

mostly i grieve for felix's suffering. it is almost overwhelming to behold him in pain or distress, and knowing that he has no power to move through it on his terms, and i have no power to make it better is agonizing. much to let go of today.

blessings to you all, m

I had to do what he could not but i had no idea how or what. Events outstripped my knowledge and outpaced the deep wisdom i was lucky to glimpse. I grieved a parent's grief.

THE MINISTRY OF LOVE

I have been driven many times upon my knees by the overwhelming conviction that I had nowhere else to go.

ABRAHAM LINCOLN

SAME WEEKEND

Feeling-states burst inside me like fireworks. Was i meant to feel sad? Did I gain advantage for having, and noticing my own emotions? Being in the vicinity of death affected everything.

Tina was in constant grieving and i was close behind. We were mostly out of touch with each other. I was bunkered at the hospital, she was sheltered in a small nook at Melody's house. There wasn't much to say. We both knew.

***

Grieving was a choppy earthquake that undulated my whole landscape. I could see it coming from far horizon, a cataclysmic ripple racing unstoppably toward me. Grief arrived with no warning that i could discern—flash! then deluge!!

Yet, i began to perceive qualities of grief i had missed in all my sadness, her ancient femaleness, her endless love for me and all of us, her patience. She was elder, bound here simply to help us through the darkness. She insisted I come gently.

***

Sunday early morning i escaped ICU as my mom arrived from Los Angeles to fill the bedside seat. I fled the incredible pain of Felix's room and walked head-down, in gales of solitude along the paths and roadways of least avoidance. I resisted not. I avoided all eyes for my eyes marked me as someone apart.

Regularly i slowed, succumbed and, pushed down by deep gravity, surrendered my will to compliance. I came to my knees and sobbed, and held on to anything solid as my body convulsed and anguish deepened.

My muscles obeyed ancient instruction and bent me in on myself and pulled my head up so i could wheeze in, then down again to shake in rhythm, and breathe me out.

***

I had no choice, i was a boy-man enduring too much sadness, lost in a biological soul process deeper than anything i could choose to accept or refuse. Nothing stopped Grief as she drenched me in the open embrace of her compassion. I wrote:

> sunday morning. so many emotions roil through me. deep feeling for felix's suffering. longing for something closer to normal. deep feeling for hanna and saskia and the long road ahead for them. deep feeling for tina's grieving...

> one of the hardest parts is knowing that life goes on, and that i will need to re-enter that stream, no matter how all this unfurls. i will need to work, and raise the girls, and make plans for the future.

> life is a trip. there is no security. it's not a fairy tale... i'm feeling so trite, but all the cliche's are real it seems.

I had learned that life on earth is not supposed to be paradise. We're here to journey the sinewy rope-bridge between joy and suffering, beauty and madness and not succumb, until we choose otherwise.

> right now, it's hard to imagine a deep smile will ever return to my soul, but probably it will. it's always been like that.

> one thing i have to hold onto is that the times in my life that have brought me greatest gladness have been time with my family and community, times when i have found stillness and divinity, and times when i've been able to be of service. those

paths are still open to me, so somehow through this dark valley, there is a way.

if not paradise here, then what? to learn, i believe. to learn what? how to behave? how to love in the face of great pain? how to reconnect with deeper meanings rather than superficial pleasures? how to treat everyone with kindness, love and compassion?

when saskia was born, i remember the first few days taking times to simply look into each other's eyes. i felt i could see her soul, unadulterated by time, suffering and desire. i felt that she came from a pristine place, and i have always drawn comfort from that. whatever was before this life, and whatever comes after, i believe, will not be hell. it will be a place with fewer veils between us and the Divine....

have a blessed, amazing, sacred, precious day, m

I wrote to stay sane, to make sense, to give back. People replied, opened themselves to our pain and in so doing let us know that they would go anywhere with us, as far as we needed. We were a vast sea striving to inundate endless oceans with our Love.

***

I felt peoples' words deeply, even if i could not read them at the time; they were hands that cradled my elbow as i pushed myself off the pavement, hands that would help me no matter what. Simple prayers from deep places rang true; i was nourished when Samantha wrote:

> *Your words hold a painful beauty and your insights are profound. We're on this journey with you. We are crying with you as we read and think about sweet Felix... and the tears save us from being burnt to the ground.*

We evolved our collective knowing and shared ways to see common experience. Prayers accumulated and took on spiritual mass. They influenced our lives and illuminated for us safe passage, tiny candles dotting the valley floor...

> *You are all in our thoughts and we wish you to feel the support and empathy flowing from your community. May it sustain you while you and Felix recover from this life changing experience. Love is all there truly is. At the core of your fear and grief, may you find that love and be at peace.*

That was the crazy miracle of it all. At the core of this tragedy i truly felt Life's greatest Love!

Go With Grief When She Comes

Grief forced me to breathe so deep that i was empty of everything. I sobbed out. Each inhale brought life, energy, a new beginning. Passing willingly through Grief helped me open to seeing gifts and miracles that otherwise i would have been too afraid to behold.

> sunday 10am, i broke down this morning. grief overcame me and i was overflowing with tears beyond measure. i so miss my beautiful prince. i touch his head and hold his hand and i miss him so dearly. i cannot begin to tell how deeply sad i am to be without my felix.

> i took a walk and imagined felix with me, and i prayed for his return and i watered a forest with my tears. i miss him so deeply, and this is such cruel pain. he lives, and yet i grieve for him. something has died. i know not what. but where there is life there is hope.

> there is no closure. he has surprised us before; it's his battle most of all and he is strong and young. these words are a lifeline for me now. i feel less alone.

Grief was extraordinary, all consuming, sad, insistent but not cruel. She was best taken quickly. Grief asked only for total submission. In return, peace, many breaths where Beauty was seen again.

> this has definitely been the saddest 24 hours of my life. 44 years, and these have been the most filled with grief.

> i am struggling to notice in myself that i feel i am letting go, that part of my grief involves detaching myself from felix and his life. i have put every ounce of energy into his healing this past week, and it feels that all that has gone nowhere. i am afraid he is not coming back. i am in mourning.

> i'm sure this is selfish. i think i'm protecting myself. i don't know. my mom is coming today to stay w/ us for a week, and she will sit with felix. some friends have offered as well to simply be present.

> i do not dread the recovery process, the rehab. i just don't know where to start. there is so little to go on right now. we're still waiting for some sort of signal as to what comes next.

i feel i must maintain vigil, but i am so deeply fatigued, and i know the girls need their dad at least somewhat intact for the days and months ahead, so i cannot retreat.

grief can be so crushing. it is only endurable b/c it does not kill me, and hence, i must bear it.

one day... this will not last forever... nothing does.

blessings, m

Grief came to me ancient, female, deeply caring but firm. I went with her as a little child goes trembling hand-in-hand with a seemingly mirthless elder. She shepherded me through scary places and reassured my full, trembling self that all was totally ok.

With my every wracking sob, Grief opened herself to me: come in, she said, i'll give you shelter from the storm. A poem came later, *The Invitation* by Oriah Mountain Dreamer. It spoke to me in words of Grief herself:

> *It doesn't interest me what you do for a living.*
> *I want to know what you ache for*
> *and if you dare to dream of meeting your heart's longing.*
>
> *It doesn't interest me how old you are.*
> *I want to know if you will risk looking like a fool*
> *for love*
> *for your dream*
> *for the adventure of being alive.*

She wanted to know if i had touched the center of my own sorrow, if i had been opened by life's betrayals.

> *I want to know if you can sit with pain*
> *mine or your own*
> *without moving to hide it*
> *or fade it*
> *or fix it.*

To sit with pain was my task. I was Grief's companion. In return she gave me Beauty, and made everything less grim. I surrendered fully and accepted her invitation as gracefully as i could. There was no burden. There was only sadness falling away like autumn leaves hurried off by a relentless October wind.

Ministry of Love

Tina wrote, in deep pain, days later:

> Thank you again for all your thoughts and love— reading your words is like therapy for me. When i leave Felix's side after being with him for a day and a night to go home with the girls i walk into an emptiness that is oddly filled with sound and movement, traffic and lights.
>
> I don't know how to be in the world, how to talk to people or meet their eyes, and i don't know how to be home either. After getting back to the place that i've been calling home for the past 10 years, I start straightening up the house while the girls play.
>
> Periodically i run into something Felix has made or touched— his piano notes, a big Erector set crane, the sandals he climbed the tree with... and i don't know what to make out of it. I'm moving around the house without inhabiting it, until i sit down, and read the website, and cry. I cry for all the hope and love you send our way, and i cry for the fear of optimism. I cry because i want to believe, and i'm afraid to believe.
>
> I've been reading The Aquarian Gospel of Jesus The Christ next to Felix's bed side for the past 2 weeks— a book Mark had introduced to me years and years ago as something i absolutely must read, but i never got to it. Now it brings me comfort and solace. Here is a passage i recently read and come back to often:
>
> 'Why should you weep? Tears cannot conquer grief. There is no power in grief to mend a broken heart. The plane of grief is idleness; the busy soul can never grieve; it has no time to grief. When grieving comes trooping through your heart, just lose yourself; plunge deep into the ministry of love, and grief is not.'
>
> Plunge deep into the ministry of love, and grief is not.
>
> love, tina

bear up

inside

all was not one,
for despair
had come from outside
and beyond...

cells felt
the antithesis of
all Life... the awful place
where none remember
the sheer grandeur
of being alive.

***

Valiant ones
abhorred
vascular funerals
that slowed
the going on
about the business
of keeping death at bay.

Behold.

Many showed up to
repair
renew
restore,
but many did not;

they mourned
or gave up too soon,

while self
the vibrant one,
extended only
as far as perception—beyond,
everything was dark.

***

Felix cells
were optimistic
by nature,

but right then
they sensed
with stunned silence
the vastness
of all eternity;

they watched
as dread
lodged in the
shadow of
the Spark of Love.

***

Catastrophe was rife,
as were
resilient meadows
of regeneration.

Flesh grew whole
inside tactile mitosis

as green shoots
of new life
pressed
toward the
outlasting sun.

The body
intended
for each contingency...

cells no older
than ten short years
mended, patched
and rebuilt,
while heavy chemicals
flooded tissue
so fast
that i could feel
nothing
but sad.

My son's mind-soul
was a debris-field
in all directions,

a beaten egg
dropped in
fast boiling water.

BEHOLDING

STILL

No harbor was safe; i was adrift on a vast ocean. I dodged dread while i co-existed with hours, and Sunday morning i handed care of Felix to Tina and my mom. I left the hospital as our neighbor Nanci arrived and i stumbled downhill toward Portland below. The sunlight was alien, as if i'd landed on a faraway planet drifting around a foreign star. I survived as i could, and to endure i wrote:

> sunday. oh my god the grieving is so intense. there is nowhere to escape from it.

> i left felix at the hospital w/ my mom and nanci our dear neighbor. now i am in portland, and it is so so hard. i can't go anywhere without remembering a time i was there with felix.

> the beautiful baby next to me at this cafe i cannot bear to look at. i could drive or walk all night and day and night and still not break free. hence, i endure. it is so hard.

> be strong in your families.

Every moment, every sensation, every movement felt bleak. The sadness was beyond. Storm clouds engulfed me, but the eye of the hurricane was blind and without calm. I sobbed till i was empty.

I slid down a dirt-clod slope toward sad old age. Gravity pulled, then a crack, not of lightening, but in the matte of insatiable darkness. A rift in the pain opened and with timeless ease, serene light shined into my soul.

***

The sky was half overcast, grays and whites painting themselves on wet, slow moving clouds. I had just fled crying yet another family café that reminded me too much.

I walked aimless, unforeseen, when a light from miles above caught my eye and cast my gaze over the trees to see sunshine knifing through a rip in the hazy clouds.

A sacred, magical slash rayed through and all was still. Fear was uprooted and i experienced total peace.

***

I was invited to pay attention, to notice how to beget all love. Rapt, i was content.

Loving warmth vibrated me and reset my elemental cells. All was perfect.

Twenty seconds of this, thirty, then poof, snow powder gone, but i was changed. True reality—even if just a likeness—is more powerful than death itself. We are safe. It is, and always will be OK.

***

Stripped bare, nowhere to hide, i was touched by, and touched Divine Grace—which is real and living—and can only come from a Loving God who long ago dreamed up mercy for we billions who suffer. One drop in a sea of sadness but enough, and enough is plenty.

***

I was cradled by Grace for hours, but did not defer my eternal vigil.

> i have been crying and praying and putting one foot in front of the other. grief had been ceaseless, and then i felt an opening, and the presence of divine grace.

it was in small measure a counter to the bottomless sadness. i remembered that felix is alive, that he lives in his injured body, that no one knows what will happen with him and this life.

i remembered to remember how little we really know about what we're here for, and i felt a sense of peace, however fleeting, that this is not the devastating end for us, that no matter what, the prayers and support and love and hopes and joy that surround us and have infused our lives for years, they all matter. they are real and powerful and true and that somehow, in the end, good will prevail.

***

when i think of felix, i know it's his innate kindness and love and humor that have touched so many of you and given you seeds to support us.

amidst this tragedy there is so much to be thankful for, and for now, i'm just grateful for one small window into that truth.

grief is not done with us, the suffering might grow deeper, but in the end, the sadness will not consume us, the pain will not defeat us, and somehow, life and love will continue.

***

That glimpse did not mean that Felix would live. If he lived, he might not think. Grace did not replace my yearnings for Felix to overcome, but she companioned me as i walked through the valleys of darkness.

***

Grace, yes and more, and in the calm after-storms i was cleansed; despair ebbed and i better perceived everything.

Grief was satiable and created space in the pain, gaps when the relentless fear of forever losing my son gave way to something bigger, something easily encompassing all of everything. Grace blossomed in the cracks of the unyielding.

***

There was deep acceptance in ICU amid long moments of true calm, and washed bare i surrendered. I saw opportunities—the edge i had so earnestly been seeking. Faith's hard seed cracked open and from the thistles a sacred *yes!* burst out through the barbs of my cluttered mind.

Do not be afraid *child*, you are not alone. God, Love, Grace, Beauty, Joy... all good remains. I saw past illusions of permanence that had long fertilized my attachment to suffering and i realized, across trillions of cells, that Life is perfect just as it is.

***

The experience was too much to contain, so i wrote:

> God, if i can serve You by helping those who must walk in the Valley of the Shadow, please help me make it so.
>
> I want to be an angel along that road, one who helps those in deepest despair to see your Light.

***

Grace let me sip from her cup but it was double-edged; i needed comfort, and i had work to do. I was a tired man stumbling along uneven sidewalks, tears streaming out my eyes. I searched for only one thing, a way out, but none was visible.

I was confused, praying, seeking—open to whatever fates might spare me. I believed there was a way through the pain, though i knew that way might not include Felix's continued participation in life.

With one last glance at the sky above i accepted earth, and pain, and returned to the hospital to help my seemingly dying son.

At the Edge of Gravity

I had a hard time being fearless. I drifted on my pain, mourning in advance, present only to my own suffering. I was tempted to be consumed entirely.

My present tense was a comatose haze where i made space in my heart for attending Felix's last breath. I vowed to take whatever edge my beloved son might need, endure any passage fully present, serving Felix as best i could.

I would show up without fear, filled with vastest Love. I would do anything so his last moments here would be safe and awesome. It hurt so to imagine this, but i needed to be ready just in case.

***

When grief, mourning and somber preparation had their time, i intervened on our behalf. I sought ways to change the fast-seeming course of our lives.

While Felix still breathed i had to show up and keep looking! Grace had given me courage to persevere, and that gift i had to nourish as if our lives depended on it.

To the quiet rhythm of ICU i returned Sunday afternoon, the warmth of Grace cupped in my empty hands, hauling last drops of water to my deep-thirsting son.

A CARDINAL TASK

The dark background which death supplies brings out the tender colors of life in all their purity.

GEORGE SANTAYANA

SUNDAY...MONDAY

Ten minutes back in ICU and i was parched. Grace left while i had my back turned and i felt an inkling—from across far-time—of an ancient father's task, but i couldn't see it. I was drained and small, too blind through tears to behold the one light in the darkness that might draw us home.

Exhausted, i could not sit still; i hacked at brambles to put right all that was broken. Nothing. I squirmed in depleted agony.

***

Sunday afternoon Tina returned to work at Felix's bedside after 53 hours; i was pummeled. I needed rest even more than i needed to tend my son, so i gathered the girls and we left the hospital, and left Felix in the loving care of his mother and grandmother.

I needed my daughters' unbroken attention. I needed parts of my life that worked, tasks i could complete, small successes like picking out a movie and making dinner without burning anything down.

I longed for a four year old's pronouncements and an eight year old's wisdom. Hanna, Saskia and i took ourselves home, closed the door, and lived the next 16 hours alone together on Grant street.

I devoted myself entirely to their wellbeing and directed all the love that had engulfed me toward them. I let their love spill back over me and found hours of peace—oases amid the desolation.

A Way Back

Monday first-light i felt only pain—pain i didn't know how to fend off. Grace was elsewhere. I dropped the girls at a summer school that a dear friend had donated, and headed to the hospital. I was unstill.

I clutched at the belief that every moment i remained grateful would keep demise at bay. I made good thoughts like a child pats together cakes of mud. I tried to breathe, to remember Joy, and i vowed not to turn and flee.

> the grief is so intense. it is so consuming when it comes. i cannot walk with it. i cannot do anything but let it have its way.
>
> Felix is relatively unchanged. small movements of his limbs, perhaps his eyes. i still feel him in there though, and i tell him over and over that i love him, that his sisters are well, that i'm taking care of his family the best i can.

In reality, i was convinced any good sign was hallucination; it lessened the risk to my soul. People showed up to vigil with us and their experience influenced ours; they too, grieved in the darkest hours:

> *Although I barely know you, this tragedy and the grace and authenticity with which Mark has shared this experience has impacted me like no other event that I can remember. Every day I look at Felix's beautiful face on this website as I pray and say grace, (a rare occurrence for an agnostic, buddhist jew).*
>
> *I experience such powerful pain and sadness as I listen and read. Tears pour from my eyes that have never been able to produce tears, only dry seized up sobs. -j*

I practiced non-blinking and tried to reflect.

What Would Felix Have Me Do?

The agony stabbed at me from inside and i threshed to find ease. Felix was crippled in his coma, teetering, and i worried for his death. I worried too, for his survival.

I started with what i knew: i was Felix's father. That remained. I was his only father, and he was my only son. I needed to parent, and whatever it was that i was called to do, would be as Felix's dad. Words drained the terror:

> monday, my thoughts turn to how best to keep faith with this. the grief and the sorrow are so huge; i cannot better hold them at bay than i could the surging of an ocean flood.
>
> i worry that he may need care his whole life, and i worry who will care for him when i am old and dying.
>
> it's maddening. i worry that such worry will dampen possibilities for his recovery. i worry that worry is a cancer that will seep into our beings and wash away any real hope for rebirth.
>
> i wonder how to keep faith with Felix, and i wonder how to keep faith with life.
>
> ***
>
> even so, i have found a path. during the dark hours when grief first arrived and would not leave—could not be vanquished with logic or prayer or love or any other power i could bring to bear —when that grief came and crushed me down and brought me more pain and sadness than i ever knew one person could bear, i was given a moment of grace.
>
> grief paused.
>
> grief is not kin to fear or evil, but is simply sadness multiplied larger than a thousand oceans.
>
> grief demands full attention, nothing less, but she is not mean.
>
> when i prayed on my knees—unable to stand—prayed for some hope, for something that was not grief, for a way forward that was not utter, inconsolable, desolate sadness, when i so asked every great spirit and angel of the Divine—grief parted, and allowed ancient kin to visit me.
>
> comfort came, and as the 23d psalm promises, i was not alone. i was not companioned to fear or evil, but was allowed to know that i was tethered still to love, to life's most blessed joys, to a vista of days to come that were not inundated with sadness, but promised to be filled again with happiness—real, grounded, sincere, breathing happiness.

when that grace came, i stepped into it, hungrily yes, but more to witness what it was, more to see what i could bring with me from that place, to find some knowing that i could carry into the grief ahead. it wasn't immediate, but today i found a key left for me by grace. i asked myself the question: what would Felix want me to do now?

the answer was clear. he would want me to care for his sisters, and make sure that they grow up with joy and love and hope, and not immersed in grief without end. he would want me to care for his mother so that her suffering can ease enough for the love to seep back in and salve the pain.

he would want me to keep the family strong; he would want me to laugh and tell stories and smile and have hope and see the best in the world. he would want me to never, ever stop loving him, or his sisters or his mom or his extended family.

he would say to me that he is healing right now, and he can't be there to help me with that, but he would say very sweetly that i know what to do, that i had shared all that with him and that he loved me and was proud of me.

***

when the grief comes, i let it come. i let it wash over me, but after a time, when its mighty waves ebb and i am left exhausted on the shore, i pick myself up, dry my eyes, and move back into the world, with love in my heart, for Felix.

With love in my heart for everyone.

LEARNING TO LISTEN

Pulling myself forward through the fog did not eliminate the risk of plunging off the cliff, but with the chance of Love at hand at least i had my next breath. I took care of Felix's family as best i could, for he needed a strong family to come home to.

Tina was beleaguered but the girls kept one foot in childhood and welcomed me to share with them the sweetness of their innocence.

A rhythm emerged: spend 30 hours at the hospital—part of that with the girls but mostly alone with Felix, or talking with his mom or querying the staff about what might be. We were fully in our roles: Tina was 'mom' and i was 'dad, suffering'. We both were. Then 18 hours at home with Saskia and Hanna, exist. Repeat.

monday, day 10, this morning, hanna said that we all needed to be extra strong, b/c Felix needs to be surrounded with strength and love, and we had to help make that for him. she is so very wise. i am so blessed to be with her.

WITHOUT DISTRACTION

Gratitude and i found me a way to help Saskia: be her dad; then she feels grateful.

it is so easy to be filled with grief every second, but grief doesn't demand total surrender like fear. grief is kind in her way, but ever so persistent. she lets you take breaks, and does not want to kill you. when called, it is simply her nature to take you to the place of deep sadness and be there with you. you must go when she calls. that's the hard part.

by simply being with saskia, appreciating her funny comments, picking up on her subtle calls to engage in playful imagination, admiring her elegant demeanor or clothes... if i can do that, be with her fully, without distraction in those moments when i am washed bare from the crying, then she feels that at least part of her world is right and normal and stable.

we all ask for what we need. the trick, is to learn how to listen.

IT'S WORSE

Through this warped nightmare an hour of torment was eternity. Saskia wouldn't go upstairs alone in our house.

monday, in case any of you were wondering if this is as bad as the 'nightmare' we have all feared for our children. no, it's worse, so much worse. the pain and anguish are without depth, the sadness is only bearable b/c it refuses to kill me and i am left without choice. the worst, the part i didn't see coming, is how it never ends. this nightmare continues.

sleep truly brings relief. i was having a dream a couple of nights ago, and was so sad to wake up, b/c what had been a time without sadness was replaced by this story, this life, where Felix really is severely injured, where our family really is wounded deeply, and where untouched joy is a distant memory.

take care of your loved ones. there is no security in life. none of us knows what is to come. at times, that is hard to bear, but for

> now, i can hold out small hopes every day b/c there is nothing
> left to fear.
>
> we've already been to the valley of the shadow of death. i can
> still pray for Felix's recovery. i can still believe in miracles.

***

I paused, and certainly wept on my fingers...

> back to this moment. these words, and your taking time to read
> them, helps me immeasurably.
>
> back to breathing, in and breathing out, putting one foot ahead
> of the next, digging deep to find the seeds of smiles to share w/
> my girls. blessings to you all, m

By enduring Grief without fight, i was open to witnessing Grace. By witnessing Grace, i knew there was real Hope—not mere figments, but the promise that not all joy and love had been extinguished. This hope did not require that i hold equal space for fear.

I lifted my head up off my chest and gently wiped my eyes so that i could see again. Unblind, i caught sight of a path i hadn't noticed before, a simple road forward through the desert of unforgiving thorns.

Or maybe i made that up, like young children, and Grace without explanation took my hand and showed me a way home.

through stout vines

thoughts and memories
climbed,

whizzed by each other
and dodged collision
while waves crashed through
from outside
and walls of energy
that had long protected
gave way.

Negotiator cells
jumped to outer reaches
and extolled
the sunny virtues
of life on earth
to a boy
who might never talk again.

They over-sold,
cajoled, begged
and extracted from
wreckage-strewn thoughts
filaments
of possibility

which they hurled
back toward the
bolted skull
we loved so much.

***

Death was eternal eclipse,
a transit that would
stop mid-passage
and block light forever.

***

We careened,
and pivoted on
that one precious now
when bloomed
the notion
that
all is Good.

That above all else
sustained me.

That
and momentum.

I had no choice...
the hubbub continued.

***

Each cell
awaited clear edict
that spoke aloud
the words we longed to hear:
please,
all is well.

The Silence,

in the meantime
was profound.

FAR ENOUGH

Healing happens in the space between our breaths.

B. ALLEN, PORTLAND, OR

MONDAY, JUNE 10

I had to believe everything was right just as it was. I had to keep showing up, no matter. I was constantly pulled into the eternal glacier of my son's death but not asked to merge with it. Monday continued with un-abated sadness.

CAN THE BLACKBERRY REMEMBER?

A shaman, when asked that weekend, described seeing Felix barely tethered to this world, a soul drifting a great distance apart. Another healer reached Felix's deep spirit and told of a similar dark chasm. We all felt it, as if watching the last lifeline being sheered clean through.

> how far in advance do you think a flower knows before it blooms? does the blackberry remember over winter the bounty that will explode from its limbs come summer?
>
> i ask, b/c i found myself slipping into hope again, the lush, green lively kind, and the only way i could ground myself away from that treacherous slope was to be present with real trees and vines and flowering bushes. i walked and beheld a dance of hopes stringing themselves along the pathway like a ballroom full of lovely ladies waiting with white gloved hands for the music and dancing to begin.

I had already allowed myself to dream that we might make music again when Grief came and said slow down; i could taste from hope, but briefly. Sitting in the car i noted:

> i was weeping... i grieve most copiously in private—it's already so deeply lonely that the absence of any companionship seems to render the sadness all the more clear and sharp.

> i was weeping for i kept repeating out loud to Felix, that "we're not done you and me. we're not done my Prince."

> i said it over and over again...

***

Decisions did not ruminate that Monday; they appeared whole or not at all. I was too rushed to contemplate. Earlier that day i was driving around Portland to get food or lost or the girls when suddenly i needed to speed back to the hospital and talk to Felix.

At once, i pulled the car over and closed my eyes and reached out to him over the great distance; i called and spoke directly from my heart to his: come home, please.

You've got to come home, Prince. Now!

SIZE IS RELATIVE

I felt small. I focused all my will and the completeness of my being on the sole task at hand, as if i had been lost in a cave groping the rough walls when suddenly a dim light appeared... the lost light showing me a way out of eternal darkness.

If i showed up to this fully and without guile, if i surrendered and yet loved, we would triumph. We might not all survive or walk again, but it was a new kind of *OK*, stronger than any i had known before.

Cradling this slender hope, after silence, i hurried uphill to tell him in person. This had to come from me. I had to imbue all my earnestness, all my paternal power, all the deep and old love that Felix and i had shared since i first held him in my arms, into this one call.

I had to tell him it was time to come home.

WIELDING THE PRAYERS

I parked, moved quickly, and swept into his room feeling urgent. Like a mime, i pulled from the ethers sheaves of blessed prayers that had been hurled our way and wove them to a single fiber, drew upon every right step i had ever taken, every iota of fathers' grace i had earned in that amazing decade since i became a parent, and i gave nothing less than everything i had:

> i told him as i drove up the hill that when he gets better, we're going to have a huge party and invite all of you, and we're going to raise money to buy a piano for the cancer kids at OHSU.

> we're going to get people to come and play for the kids on that piano, and get people to come and teach the kids how to play für elise by beethoven, which was Felix's first song. i suspect i'll never hear that again without having to stop and sob.

I gave us a storyline, a plot, something we could do together. We were going to play piano for the sick kids, as soon as he got home, and better. We just had to get there first.

***

When Felix was 15 months old, the two of us were exploring an empty schoolyard in NE Portland. After running in joyous circles he started walking north, away from me. He wasn't hurrying or upset in any way. He just felt like walking.

From the center of the playground circle i watched him get smaller in the distance as the slant of the sun grew deeper. He didn't even look back. I had my life to live and he had his and was living it. His own young flesh was afoot, and far away.

Finally i called to him to come back and he turned, almost surprised that i was standing there—that i existed at all—and he toddled back to my grateful arms.

***

Monday evening was my shift, and i returned to ICU muddied. I dragged behind me the mighty sword of peoples' love, and eyes bloodshot, i vowed to battle on my son's behalf. I gave myself one cardinal task and believed i had but one shot at our survival. I believed he was contemplating the great release, his spirit far away beholding death. I had to speak up and it had to be now! My throat was scratchy from telling him how much i loved him.

I was lost for words when suddenly, calling Felix home became the prayer i had to manifest with all my will. It became the action that imbued my every breath, and it was for this i knew i had stayed alert to every intent. I had many times before prayed that an opportunity would arise when i could be of use. This was that chance.

I directed the tip of our sword. I joined together myriad strands of healing energy with my own summons, and from every cell of my vitality—whether found, felt or imagined—i distilled the spirits of attentive, earnest people and concentrated our Love. I struck, and called my son home.

***

Nothing happened. Self-serving perhaps, i pled to a prodigal boy who had roamed too far in his daring adventure, a dear child who had stepped off the end of the world and seemed to be drifting into the cold, slow embrace of death. I urged, practically ordered him to come home!

I sculpted my voice and called as if he were a two year old who had ambled too close to the edge of a busy street.

I summoned him with tears in my eyes, as if it were decades from now and he was the 44 year old father and i the old man who hoped to see my son one more time before i died.

***

Everyone called, each adding heft to our plea. One woman wrote a prayer from many hearts:

> *Sweet, sweet boy... come back to your sisters, who need their big brother around to laugh, wrestle, tease and look at bugs under logs with. Come back to your Mom and Dad who need to pack your lunch for school, make sure you have clean underwear and feel your beautiful warm arms around them. Come back to your friends who need to run through the hallway with you, empty the paint water and hear your laugh come through your smile. Come back sweet boy, come back to the people who love you. -s*

We were selfish; we wanted what we wanted. Details mattered, as did warrior intensity:

sweet Felix, we will not settle for feeling your spirit in the wind... we want you here in this world for many years to come. Please continue your healing work, and when you are ready, come back to us—to make mischief and music, let your love shine, and spend your allowance on ice cream for your sisters. -a

I called to him, yet only stillness moved. We were vast, but the universe was vaster still.

ALL IN

MONDAY, LATE NIGHT

I made my call then sat back. Five minutes, ten; no change. A new nurse came to cover for the primary who was going on break. We chatted briefly, then i tried to read but put my book down.

I waited for obvious shifts but no trumpets blared. I checked an insurance thing and asked the charge nurse about tests and mid-week schedules. I drank juice. I got coffee i didn't want. I thought about french fries or the daily special. I wondered what Hanna and Saskia were doing; i called. They were playing. It did not lift my spirits.

With no discernible ripple in Felix's essence, i challenged myself to find acceptable whatever came.

I questioned: what right did i have to call my son home? Maybe he had other missions; maybe it was his time to die, leave this place and do something else.

I strayed toward the tender colors of release, but instead doubled down on being his dad. My instincts to fight for the survival of my son overrode everything else.

ASTRIDE HUMILITY

Another question arose: what right did i have *not* to call my son back? What if Felix was lost in that fuzzy place and wanted only and totally to come home. I *had* to call, i had no doubt. I held his hand and tried not to wait.

> i had my hope, my far off dream of one day listening to my son play piano; when other hopes started kicking off their shoes and trying to dance with me, i had to be firm. i had to stay present. i had to come back to this moment, and remember that Felix is still gravely down, is still unable to speak or feed himself or move with any volition.

> i'll be here again at the hospital all night, and i cannot survive on hope. i can only survive on breath, one deep inhale, a pause, a full cleansing exhale, another pause, and then repeat. me and Felix, breathing in and out together. that's all we have tonight. and that will have to be enough.

GRIEF'S COMPANION

Grieving did not stop once i called Felix home. There was no sudden flick to mark the shift from drifting away to coming back. There was stillness—as there always is—but i was too dim to perceive it.

Monday night was quiet at the hospital. I sat, i stood at his bedside, i made my rounds about the ICU. I wrote:

> monday, before i wind up for now, i wanted to ask if any of you know who is grief's companion? i see clearly how fear and hope are intertwined.

> what about grief, which i see as a deeper being?? perhaps faith? perhaps when grief obliterates whatever in your life is not real, all that it leaves is faith.

> faith in what? i guess that's the lifelong question? i can't make it through these days without faith.

> i know some people believe that none of this matters. that we're nothing more than flesh and bones.

> i choose to believe there's more, that Love matters, and that's enough for now. Love and Felix. Felix and Love. that's my nighttime prayer, Love and Felix. Felix and Love....

I warmed myself in words; be well, i thought.

***

Combat-ready, amped on adrenaline i was barely able not to move. I leaned in to each moment, every word from the doctor and each breath of the machine. I was ready to face down all predators.

Nothing.

I was not in control. My todo list was empty.

Frustrated, i tracked the bundles of high-flying love-energy that accelerated our way, each a palpable gift of insurmountable magnitude. Helper spirits shoved back demons while children cradled sly flames of un-dimmable illumination.

When that failed to hold my attention, i went back to ferreting out salvation.

QUIET INTERCEDES

From all over, words...

> *monday afternoon 3:56pm, i am grateful for the community of family and friends that are weaving their prayers together into a big blanket of protection for Felix and our whole family. And I'm thankful for your willingness to share your journey with us. Both are great gifts. Sending healing light... -d*

> *(14 minutes later)— Felix is the embodiment of vibrance. He is one of the most radiant, robust children I have ever met. I cannot fathom him not pulling through this. -c*

The waves kept coming:

> *5:21pm - Dear Lilly Family, You are constant in the thoughts of our family... and we wish with all our hearts for a good outcome. -j*

> *6:15pm - You are in our hearts, minds, and prayers. -m*

> *8:25pm - You and your family are in our prayers right now. We think about Felix every day. With love and hope -s*

> *9:07pm - All the love and light we can send we are sending tonight. May the Source touch your family with love. -t*

> *10:49pm - Thank you for being so vulnerable and transparent in your writing, I will slow down, hug kids, be in the present and thank the present and all that is for your family. I am in awe of the beauty and teaching that is born from such pain. -r*

People stayed up with us through the night:

> *11:51pm - Tina, you have guided so many women in their pregnancies and in the many transitions of motherhood. You have listened patiently to our fears, our complaints, our joys... Now let us nourish you and your family with our love and prayers, just as you have nourished us. Love to your whole beautiful family -a*

> *11:54pm - Dear Mark, Your writing is full of such great strength and wisdom. In Chinese Medicine there is an idea that the companion of grief is the ability to receive life. Your grief calls us all to create strength and send it to your son, Felix. We are all with you. Love is Felix, Felix is love. -c*

> *tuesday, 01:44am - Dear Felix, There is more love for you, waiting for you than you ever could have imagined. -h*

***

As Monday waned i wanted to remain awake forever. If these were the last moments of Felix's life i craved to be there unblinking.

> *03:40am - The counterpart to grief is joy. Felix is joy. Even his name alludes to joy.*

> *I am a great admirer of faith. Faith is the richer cousin of hope. Faith is necessary and good. But to answer your question directly and literally, Mark, the counterpart to grief is joy. Joy is to grief as hope is to fear.*

> *Felix is a joyous child. He is and always will be a joyous child.*

> *We hold Felix in our hearts. And our hearts are breaking. Our hearts are so full with the joy of Felix, so alive with the bright flame of his life, our poor hearts can only break under the weight of such tremendous joy.*

> *Good god, let our hearts break 80 or 90 years from now.*

> *We carry you all in our hearts. We are your neighbors still in joy and grief. We are grateful and infinitely richer for the days when our home was graced with the spirit of your children, when the swings swang in the back yard and the mulberries beckoned for a dancing partner.*

Felix, come home. The world is richer with you in it. Your whole life lies before you, an ode to joy, and we will weep to hear it. -m

Thus held, i finally slept.

ALL TOO MUCH

Tuesday morning i awoke in a hospital fog and was instantly sad. Would-be sorcerer or not i was lonely, and shadows dogged until Tina came and my shift was over.

I was restless of the vigil, tired of watching fear bicker with serenity. Melancholy filtered every breath and no matter how much 'love' i beheld there was always more pain and gratitude to fill every season and every instant in between.

And then more. Always more.

My body needed care and i slipped hungrily into the few moments of calm that floated my way—unless i wasn't paying attention. I lived in a simple world: everyone was either in pain, remembered it or was untouched.

I decided that only those suffering right now could understand what i was going through—but we were of little use to each other. I donned a mask to fence in privacy, and shuddered inside.

***

I beheld death around corners, steps away always watching. I stood in stillness one moment looking out over the city from the sky-walk breathing and then bam! there's death next to me, surveying the same long view—half-burned cigarette dangling from his menacing hands... two tourists sipping tainted coffee at the smoky rim of a bottomless crater.

I was awkward in my vulnerability, and stalked by the domineering vibe of *brain-death!*—this one terrifying, terrible *thing* murking everywhere.

The death of Felix that i allowed myself to imagine was a proper crossing-over, an all-too soon body-transition into whatever's next. But *brain death!* good Lord! What sort of despair-filled emptiness was that?! It hurt to get close to, and in my soul i bowed low in grave humility.

TAUNTS

An ugly thought, he is merely alive. It felt dirty to think but i had to pretend even if it betrayed him, what it might feel like in case the physical trauma to his brain had already caused so much damage that no matter what happened next, it was already too late.

> tuesday afternoon, i tried beer for lunch to see if there was ease from a bottle of alcohol. not to be. the story continues....

> this is my new life, breathing in each breath while Felix lies on his back for the eleventh day in a row. he cannot get himself up. he cannot speak. how sad for the little prince to be trapped in a body that won't cooperate.

> i had once many times prayed to God that i wanted to be a vessel and conduit for Divine Light. i prayed to become a path for Compassion on this earth. this is not what i had in mind. i never ever intended for Felix to be caught in the webs i weave. i'm sorry Prince.

***

Physical therapy happened to him Tuesday when two therapists came and moved his limbs, sat him up with support from behind and encouraged him to connect body to body and mind to everything. It felt like watching CPR on a body that would never see life again.

> they asked him to squeeze their fingers and he did not comply. his brain would not receive, translate and send the message to his own hand to make that small connection with another human being.

> how much we would gain from that simple gesture of his. how bereft we are to live without it.

> you who are parents remember the first smile, the first intentional grasp of your mighty hand by tiny inchoate fingers. you'll never forget. the world stopped and started that day.

> we have gone back in time to hope that we can feel that once again with Felix, that once again his brain will reach out to us through his no longer tiny fingers to let us know that he hears us, that he misses us, that he is trying hard to come back.

> but that is not yet. we wait still. breath by breath we wait. it is excruciating.

There were glimpses, taunts i couldn't interpret. I heard whispers in the howl. He was more mobile Monday night and initiated more breaths on his own in advance of the machine's lagging beat. He grasped my fingers in what the physical therapists told me was likely just reflex—unwillful contractions of involuntary muscle.

there is no closure. who remains within Felix's bruised body? do we have to wait a lifetime to find out??

there is more to tell. i am exhausted. i need to sleep. in sleep, there will be a brief pause from this, then upon awakening, the long, long climb towards God only knows what will continue.

i have more concrete thoughts. they will follow. but for now i will leave you with Hanna's wisdom. she said, and i quote: "we need to be strong. Felix needs Strongness around him."

any strongness that you can spare is much appreciated. we need it.

blessings, m

I remained still and sought something braver to stand on than my own two feet.

eventually

something stirred,
and we were on again;
i was glad.

STANDING ON FAITH

*Death is the epitome of the truth that in each
moment we are thrust into the unknown. Here all
clinging to security is compelled to cease, and
wherever the past is dropped away and safety
abandoned, life is renewed.*

ALAN WATTS

TUESDAY

Tuesday endured the same as Monday until it didn't. Meanwhile,
within the underlying hum of my skittish existence lay a heavy girdle
about my sacral spine—first chakra, deep-dark, primal, reptilian and
last to die. Literally.

My core vibrational skeleton was fused bones of rigid-blue
stroked through with supple brush aluminum. I feared the instant it
would all harden to cold steel.

In the spaces between severe insight i willed Felix to survive. I
tried to rest and i tried to learn something useful, and sometimes i
tried to forget... which never lasted long.

Writing was self-archeology. I dug for practical knowledge that
would help us endure, and passed back discoveries to those at the
other end of the bucket brigade: *take care of your people!* i yelled.

Live as fully as you can right now, for Real! It may be gone as
quick as the final exhale of a life now over.

***

I tried to love everyone.

PLEASE!

I walked and made sense: Friday, near death. Saturday, nearer. Sunday misery, then Grace, then misery again. Monday an inspiration, a call, then bored. Tuesday i didn't dwell in majesty.

I lit a match on the beach before a growling wind. The moment slipped and no discernible change lay bare. The best path was to believe in all good things but have no expectations, and pay attention. It was not paying attention when the blind-side smashed me upside the head.

Hundreds followed us into dark alleys and confronted with us fear of the bleakest sort. They exposed themselves to our desolation.

> tuesday, knowing what i know now, the depth of anguish that is possible, the unending sadness that is my daily bread, would i trade away that incessant pain never to have known Felix at all? would i trade away the most amazing ten years of my life to be free of this forever? no. never!
>
> never in a million years would i give away one day of the time i spent with the Prince. nothing could pry from my fingers one second of loving him and being loved by him, even if i have to endure this agony for the rest of my life.
>
> please, please, love your loved ones as if you'll never see them again. love them as if this is the last day of your life together. i know you can't live like that every second, but please, please do not ever again let a day pass that you don't relish the love of your most beloved, that you don't get down on your knees and thank whatever divine spirit lives close to you for the mere privilege of sharing a day with someone who touches your soul so closely.
>
> there is an infinitely thin line between heaven and hell, and you never know when you might be asked to cross over.
>
> please.

LOVE AND COMA

Care flooded our way. People birthed Christian prayer circles, Jewish healing rituals, yogic blessing ceremonies, chantings, kirtans and pagan sacraments. Shamanistic skills imbued Buddhist gatherings, and people of all ages held private service to manifest the intense active healing energy that flew our way. One such gift came from Felix's friends at school:

Hello Felix, a group of your 3rd and 4th grade classmates and their families met tonight to hold a candlelight vigil for you at Frank's house. We stood under the big tree in front of the house, all in a circle. We all brought a candle and lit it. The flame is a symbol of life and of the soul.

Frank's Mom told us to look into the flame where we might see our guardian angels dancing in the flame. We saw them there and we asked the guardian angels to talk with your guardian angels to ask them to bring you to a safe place to heal so that you can come back to us again. We are thinking a lot about you and we miss you very much. We are so sorry about what has happened. We love you Felix.

There was raw power in each word. From the other side of town:

...everywhere I go I hear your story Felix. You are famous. This is my vision. The next place I go when I hear. "Did you hear about Felix Lilly?" I will hear, "He is awake and vibrant!!!" -s

We weren't awake, and we all so badly wanted this one ten year old boy to live but he was far from vibrant, and still fully sedated.

***

The docs would periodically stop the drugs to assess the depth of Felix's neurologic injury; we zeroed in on tiny movements and his perceived reactions to our stimuli: nothing.

I was in charge of squeezing his toe in an effort to elicit pain; i jammed my thumb desperately into his nailbed and when he didn't flinch i hurt. Questions stabbed at me like needles of glass: is Felix alive in that mind of his? What's left of his thinking brain?

I thought he was dead, at least to us—we who could talk and make eye contact. I moved through streets already worn with my footsteps.

tuesday, midday - portland is a minefield. nowhere is safe. over there, that's where Felix and i bought his baseball mitt. there's where he learned to swim and that's where we used to get chocolate.

how to live like this? i don't know. i'm making it up as i go along. i'm trying to simplify. how can i honor Felix? how can i care for his sisters? how can i create out of this sadness a beauty more powerful than the pain?

> i have been grieving so! it is intense beyond belief. i hope some-
> how these words will give you enough clues to avoid some dis-
> aster that need not be. i do not know. tragedy happens. grief is
> my muse these days. she is my insistent, kindly companion, and
> she is with me every step of the day.

ALL JOIN IN

Seeking space between the pain, i noted myriad bits which together
amounted to the case that was Felix Maus. Every time i cried and she
was near, Saskia wordlessly hugged me with all her might; Hanna
made plans for our survival while Tina grieved.

Backstories swirled—nurses holding their own unsolved grief and
doctors hiding grave personal doubts that would never be voiced
aloud; together we stood at the bedside witnessing, watching men
across the unit mourn—fathers who would grow old too soon and
never heal.

***

The people tending Felix had protocols for everything but intuition.
They practiced craft, part alchemy, part science, part making it up as
you go along.

I joined late night discussions between neurosurgeons and inten-
sivists about what to do, about hardware and medicines, elements
and restoration, while life and death lived un-discussed, remaindered
for solitary contemplation. I documented my perceptions of vaguely
passing time:

> 3:00 am... Felix's intracranial pressure spikes. What do i do?
> What would you do? You can sedate him more to calm his flail-
> ing arms and decrease his overall agitation; this hopefully will
> keep the brain from swelling more. But at some point you have
> to ween the boy off narcotics and take whatever truth careens
> your way. What to do then?

Too much mass was trying to fit in too small a space. His ICP's hovered in the mid-40's and nothing else mattered. The measurements
stated that his brain was swelling and would, if current trajectories
continued, explode.

I felt him dying to me each oxygen-starved moment, as if i were
beholding the end-stage violence of his brain clambering down the
back of his skull toward a final rupturing blowout.

SWERVE

Then a shift—subtle yes, and quiet—but unnoticed. I did not in re-al-time behold that precious inflection when he turned home, but it happened. That's all that matters. We weren't going to die, at least not this week—not in ICU.

UNSCREWING

Tuesday evening the neuro-docs, in consultation, removed Felix's bolt; it was penned in his chart. The implication: Felix was no longer at the edge of death. We had survived.

There was nothing more the bolt could do for the boy who fell. He could still die, of course, but the scale had tipped from quite possible to probably not.

***

I imagined later a silence at the farthest reach of his travels when he stopped moving away, but hadn't yet turned for home... the pause be-tween our breaths.

With the removal of his bolt, they prepared us to leave ICU.

We didn't know if the next stop was a nursing home for weeks of tedious stasis before rehab, or if it was time to recover. All was ob-scure, but we were part-way home and still no contact with Felix. We remained far apart.

> they took felix's bolt out today. that was the device literally screwed into his skull that measured his intracranial pressure, that is, how much oxygen makes it to Felix's brain on any given heartbeat.

> the neurosurgeon decided that he was making progress, and that other staff members (RN's and overnight docs) were look-ing too much at the 'numbers' and not enough at Felix. when they looked only at the numbers, they re-sedated him too quickly.

> there's something rich in that to ponder, but it's beyond my grasp now. what it means in real terms is that we have moved into the 'recovery' phase. this lasts two years, they say, and more, with the first six months being the most crucial.

> six months of every day hoping that he grasps our hand when we ask him to, every day wondering if we have plateaued forev-

er, or if there is still some miracle buried within his marvelous soul...??

Not-dying was the giant new acceptance. Recovery meant he might be able to lift a spoon to his mouth before another ten years was out. Its pace remained opaque. How long would it take to teach Felix again simply how to say 'thank you'.

We were ignorant of his cognition, uncertain whether he would ever waken or respond. We could not tell if he would walk or speak or feed himself again, or hold a job and become a dad.

We knew nothing about the future, only the present. We were, by spoken agreement, slightly less likely to die in ICU, but beyond that it was dark void to all of us.

GREAT DISTANCE

I dropped the most heavy irons of sightless fear from about my inner self, nothing more. Medical discussions continued but i was elsewhere.

Antibiotics, arterial lines and fluid drip were too laden to keep me engaged, despite the usual incentives. What could i do, really? An invisible valley separated me from Felix—a gap we had deftly spanned with a smile days before.

> tuesday evening, we hear many stories. the one foremost in my mind today is the family whose eldest, a boy, (2 younger sisters) was in a coma for 4 months. 4 months! good lord. that is mad. that's why this whole day to day, breath by breath thing is a salvation. how else could you make it that long?
>
> also last night i read the funeral notice of a 12 year old boy who died. he was a light to all he touched. he died too soon. he left a void. he was one of the angels. how deeply i knew those words. how close we have walked to all that... all that closure.
>
> and suddenly, i breathed in. what else was there left to do but exhale, and try again. that's all we really have.

The road ahead was cratered with grave threat, and one direct truth: even if Felix survives, he may never get better than this.

BEDROCK

Faith is not something to grasp, it is a state to grow into.

M K GANDHI

TUESDAY-WEDNESDAY

Breath infiltrated my body with surprising regularity and i noticed peoples' scars; we faced more change.

They were planning our exit, alive, from ICU. I left the hospital late Tuesday to walk with Grief and knew beyond doubt that animals grieve. I thought of people a century ago picnicking in cemeteries; i could hear the grave laughter of children, and the stern admonitions of parents to be careful under the cloudy sun.

Grief swept me under her torrential cascade from which i could not get up, and i cried from the inside until only dry sobs remained.

When Grief drew back, satisfied, she didn't leave me adrift. She revealed beneath my feet a stock of eternal bedrock—Faith, upon which to rest and give thanks that it wasn't worse.

tuesday, grief's mate is faith.

not like fear and hope, those less than ethereal phantasms. grief is real. very real. and faith??? i have come to feel faith is groom to grief, a place to come back to, an answer to the question 'why?'—why am i enduring this?

have faith young son. have faith, faith that there will be mean- ing and joy and lightness again. felix and love. love and felix. it works!

After grieving i was cleansed. Lighter, i basked in her primal gift and upheld the chance to rebuild our very lives.

I stood upon Faith and knew that it would not give way or vanish. It would outlast all this, me, my pain. It was foundational, a glimpse into the super-structure of the universe, site-lines to the girders of our Love-made worlds.

In God's Image, We Create

Many wrote to share their thoughts on Grief's mate. We plumbed spiritual realms while struggling to survive this one:

> I would say that Grief's companion is Knowledge of Spirit Life. -m
>
> -
>
> Mark, I'm not an expert, but I would guess grief's companion is healing. One must work through the grief and begin to heal...not forget, but heal and go on with a purpose. Just as scar tissue is stronger, you will eventually build strength of purpose. -c
>
> -
>
> Compassion and wisdom are companions of grief. But you've already found my dearest companion in grief—presence. -c
>
> -
>
> Grief contains a quality of 'ending', a sense of 'no redemption', 'done-ness', 'never-more-ness' and a real feeling of permanent loss. Grief implies the destruction or diminishment of a former state of being. We truly miss that former 'way-it-was' situation.
>
> So, who is holding hands with Grief? It has come to me that it might be Creation. The making of something new, something worthy, something valuable and holding a presence in this world of ours. -m

Tiny Fingers

Mercy and Grace are siblings to Grief, and Love can never be extinguished while Life itself courses through our blood.

An angel told me so.

(tuesday night, late) gosh i write a lot about me. thanks for bearing with.

well, how's Felix?? tonight i came into the hospital exhausted, drained, spent, fried, and then i saw my prince.

i came next to him, and i truly believe he knew i was there.

he moved his legs and arms. he grasped my fingers. his breathing and heart rate spiked.

i so felt his presence. i feel like an angel came into my life this evening and graced me with a small miracle. a small but mighty miracle.

We had been granted a reprieve, a decision handed down. In this tiny corner of the universe a butterfly flapped its wings and new life erupted bravely through the fire-blackened hillside. It was majesty, and we were born again. I have no idea why.

***

Some things are so beautiful they only live a short instant before they flame out. The next moment arrives. Breathe slowly.

i asked the nurse if he saw it too, if he knew what i was saying, if i was hallucinating, and he said he knew what i meant and he felt it too. my mom and the nurse said after hanging out with him today they feel there is someone in there in Felix's brain.

i felt for 20 minutes that he was straining with every ounce of his being to connect with me, to answer my gentle *i love you's*— and then he was spent.

Felix was not gone! My father's joy was complete! He was in there, resting in that crazy beaten spaceship of his, reaching out and trying to connect! He exhausted himself so that we would know that he was alive.

the physical therapist today said that you ask them to do something like grasp your finger, and then you wait for 20-30 seconds because it might take that long for the message to make it from brain to fingers. then you tell them to stop, or six hours later they still might be squeezing. it's that cloudy in there.

but tonight, i do not have to look so hard to feel faith. i don't have to scrape myself off the pavement and dry my eyes and steel myself for misery again, i have a companion for the long

> hours till dawn. Felix is with me. me and Felix. Felix and popi. I
> feel very very blessed tonight.

The absolute chill was gone; an inner sun warmed me for the first
time in a hundred years.

THE STORY I TELL MYSELF

This is the story i tell myself. It lives inside a strange mix of witness,
recollection and the loose cinch of time.

I cannot tell directly what effect, if any, these prayers of ours had.
I do not know if we who pled so hard illuminated the way home for
my son, or if i have simply made all this up to give flesh to the skele-
tons of my imagination.

But verily, i do know.

It did matter. It made all the difference in the world!

We called, and Felix came home.

No parent could wish for more.

***

Had i not showed up to his bedside armed with the buoying love of so
many, i would carry with me forever an unbearable regret for what
might have been, and for what I might have done.

My striving was perhaps infinitesimal in the face of all Life but i
tried, hard. The outcome was beyond grasping, but my efforts i get to
keep.

To have been able to call Felix home, speaking sweetly into his
wounded ear, was the sword of our Love striking the bands of death
that looped around his wrists.

When i knelt down next to him at the park that one Saturday and
urged him to keep breathing, it was the millionth word in a trustful
conversation between him and me that had been running since the
day he was born.

Every time i whispered to him my love, i was topping off the cup
i'd been filling ever since i figured out years ago that Love *is* the most
potent parenting elixir. No overdose is possible.

We prayed well. Our call was clear: come back. Our job, Love. In a
vibration so familiar he heard, turned and headed home.

DEATH BLINKS

We made our finest stand.

There was no enemy, no battle waged. Thousands of blessed souls braided themselves together and hurled Love deep into blackest space.

We were a long brigade of humble people bearing torches along the bottom of the lightless valley, showing the road home for my wayward son. Months later i penned a letter:

> *Death, i write you with all humility, and if you see into my soul you know how very hard this is. I am not yet unafraid of you. I do not want to be guilty of hubris or exaggeration, but what i put down here is how i recall the events of those days in ICU, that one weekend when we danced heavily on the borderline.*
>
> *If there are any errors they are mine. If you need to call someone to account for this, it's me and only me. If you come looking for anyone in my circle of people, come looking for me; we'll talk.*
>
> *Death, you blinked. -m*

***

My deep-sight is not yet clear and death is patient, nor do i wish to trifle with Spirits. I know i was just a small man trying to grasp something that seems miraculous even today. I know what i witnessed, and i know what dwells deep within my soul.

I witnessed Felix slipping away, witnessed Tina retreating from the pain of watching her first-born edge toward death. I watched Hanna and Saskia struggle, and watched the nurses and doctors grow grim—steeling themselves for yet another child lost.

I felt the presence of death, outside of Felix's room on a small patch of floor, waiting.

I witnessed us showing up, for Felix, for ourselves, for each other. I have no doubt that had Felix fallen onto a gnarled root instead of bare ground and passed away at once, the same amazing coming together of people would have shepherded us through the grieving, the funeral, the search for meaning, the carrying on.

190 - The Boy Who Fell

We stood not so much against death—though death was clearly in our sights—but for life, for love and friendship, for families and the community that blossoms whenever people care beyond themselves.

Felix dwelt on the threshold of the great divide and we called. Death stepped back, turned away, and my boy came home.

FULLEST HEART

People showed up, a formidable tribe and prayed with fullest heart for Felix's return, and from that—and fertilized by uncountable offers to do anything, anytime—a new courage was born. We are yours.

I saw the path that might have been and it was bleak. Stand strong. Come hell-fire or emptiness, we are with you. There was nothing more i could have asked for.

***

Everything matters i knew, *every* act of kindness, every smile, and in a raw moment weeks later i wrote:

> i'll never know which prayer it was that tipped the scale, which totem for the altar strengthened the web just enough so the way home for Felix became clear.
>
> i'll never know but please never forget, that it might have been that one small gesture or prayer or offering *you* made that one scary night long ago.
>
> never ever forget that you had on angel wings last summer, and helped us call our boy home.

Thank you, everyone—and please, keep your angel wings close at hand.

AFTERWARD

INFINITY AND BEYOND

What had chilled me near death drew back. I tried to warm myself with smiles to shake loose the icy pools within, but it was celebration tinged with deepest mourning because Felix could not attend.

Not only did the reverberations of suffering still live, the pain had scraped off a blindness that revealed an acute glimpse into the torment that people can endure.

There was no after. It was, and is all now. His body lived, but his mind? We knew not. Yet, for all the tears, i was not asked to go deeper, all the way into a parent's worst nightmare.

Felix lived.

I bowed my head in exhausted gratitude.

SLUICING TOWARD QUIET

A shadow rose—not guilt about our survival—but a feeling i could not shake, that everything comes with a price.

The wonderful love i had felt was equal only to my capacity to be vulnerable to the greatest pain imaginable. Being present required holding space for dark as well as light.

I was hurtling at high rates of speed toward whatever came next, and what i couldn't hear coming was quiet. I inflected, swerved and plowed face first into the stillness of life after ICU. Death had been stayed, perhaps half a century or more, but what life would fill those years?

Light seemed far away and the Ninth Floor was next. For that, i knew naught.

step back

with ease,

behold life
becoming real
with such
ordained brilliance

and i am certain

that all is perfect
just as it is.

ACKNOWLEDGEMENTS

THANK YOU
To say i am grateful is like saying the sun provides warmth. To all, thank you, for real.

FOR STARTERS
Thank you to everyone who wrote in the online journal, who brought us food or prayed for us. Words will never tell our gratitude.

Thank you to certain places, the Irish Harp Pub (Berlin) and the Horse Brass, AudioCinema and TaborSpace in Portland, and the Multnomah County libraries. You all provided me somewhere i felt safe to write, and to be me.

Thank you to my editors Tina, Kevin, Danielle, Susan, Sue, Karen, Helen, Dani and Felix. Thank you to the folks at Caring Bridge for offering free space for me to write, and thank you to innumerable individuals including my mom, JD, my dad, Jane, John, Karin, Jeff, Jeremy, Deah, Garth, Katrina, Devon, Zita, Shawn, Tracey, Paul, Kathy, Kate, Ingrid, Sharon, Mary, Tina, Maria, Gina, Lori, Bryan, Veronica, Laura, Marsha, Nancy, Rainbow, Lauren, Bobbie, Lisa Mae, Robin, David, Jan, Nanci, Miles, Laura, Aileen, Jane, Bill, Iris, Katie, Jaime, Larry, Marnie, Fiona, Brian, Melody... and a heavenly host of others who, like so many, showed up unbidden and loved us hard.

Love Love Love!

LETTING GO

The world is full of words....

October 5, 2013, 2:27pm
I release this book with Gratitude. We survived. Others did not. That alone looms every day.

Thank you.

All Love, m

***

EVERYTHING MATTERS

Naknuwisha

Young friend,
be part of something old—
be home here in the great world
where rain wants to give you drink
where forest wants to be your house
where frogs say your name and your name
where wee birds carry your wishes far
and the sun reaches for your hand—
be home here
be healed
be well
be with us all
young friend.

KIM STAFFORD

EXCEPT FROM BOOK TWO

Healing is many things. Survival is one: keep the heart breathing, the blood flowing and the brain thinking... but in the end it's one sym-phony, and either it's playing or the theater is closed.

Healing, to use words, is everything. It's the body mending and carrying on, the obvious reclamation of wounds, but it's also the mind re-learning to walk, the arms to talk and the fingers to make music again. Yes.

But healing was more than flesh made whole that summer. It was our learning to see Love even amid the ruin of my son's brokenness. It was how i ate and how much i chewed; it was where i put my attention and what i believed was my role. It was how i showed up to everything and everyone, each moment and every heartbeat.

Healing is sensing this power we all have, and putting it to good use.

Healing was being patient, soldiering on when circumstance said give up. In the end, even when i was alone and crushed, some kind of healing continued.

Many times i forgot the feelings of Love and support that had been real hours before, and over and over again i was taken to scary places and left unable to find my way out, except by trudging through, enduring—one lone breath at a time.

***

Healing is each moment giving way to the next, each moment refreshed and new, each moment a chance to say thanks. When i forgot, it was scary. When i remembered, i was born again.

Healing is more than we can ever tell, but i'll try. I'll try to witness the majesty that surrounds us, the angels among us, the endless possibilities to Love.

For we are blessed... so much more blessed than ever we'll know.

that morning

...was it sunny inside

where uncountable cells—
focused faithfully
on Felix's ongoing existence
—showed up to tasks
they were born to...

fulfilling
the unfurling joy of
one very special
ten year old boy?

***

Begin at the last note
of this vibrant étude...

where cells outlive staid
unwielding years
then die,
as all living things will die...

then move,
post-mortem
by slow barge
to gargantuan
hepatic refineries,

where molecule by molecule
they are dismantled,
inventoried or excreted
until finally,

elements
rebuild themselves
into teeming fleshy jungles
across all the spans
of this one
wild and
precious life.

***

Carbon binds water,
weds distinct quantities
of oxidized phosphorus,
brimstone and nitrogen,

and together,
all vibrate just so
and coalesce
from chaos
into the hot wet
of living matter!

What miracle all this?

***

Pick any leaf
of his perishable
physical being
to notice...

upon waking
cells of pulmonary flesh
pull in primal concert
like earnest roots sipping
from plentiful springs,

each bent
on compelling air
into hundreds of miles
of lightless passageways...

where,
precious oxygen couplets
are herded
by the physics
of narrowing spaces
through membranes
precisely sheer
and made fast
to hemoglobin
flowing
miraculously nearby.

***

Meanwhile,
infinities away

dull air breathes out—
release,

sustenance for trees
whose limbs
will one day break
beneath
a child's carefree smile.

***